PAIN &
PRIVILEGE

SOPHIE SMITH

PAIN & PRIVILEGE

INSIDE LE TOUR

ultimo press

Published in 2022 by Ultimo Press,
an imprint of Hardie Grant Publishing

Ultimo Press
Gadigal Country
7, 45 Jones Street
Ultimo, NSW 2007
ultimopress.com.au

Ultimo Press (London)
5th & 6th Floors
52–54 Southwark Street
London SE1 1UN

Pain and Privilege
ISBN 978 1 76115 072 2 (paperback)

10 9 8 7 6 5 4 3 2 1

Cover design Alissa Dinallo
Cover photograph Russ Ellis
Typesetting Shaun Jury | Typeset in 11.5/18 pt Janson Text LT Std
Copyeditor Deonie Fiford
Proofreader Ronnie Scott

Printed and bound in Great Britain by Clays Ltd, Elcograf S.p.A.

Ultimo Press acknowledges the Traditional Owners of the country on which we
work, the Gadigal people of the Eora nation and the Wurundjeri people of the
Kulin nation, and recognises their continuing connection to the land, waters and
culture. We pay our respects to their Elders past and present.

CONTENTS

INTRODUCTION

At my first Tour de France, the sensory overload was so great that I felt like I was either drunk or hungover at the beginning.

Seventeen days before the beginning of the 2012 edition I'd packed my bags and moved from Australia to England to work at *Cycling Weekly* and *Cycle Sport* magazines.

When I landed in the UK, I knew maybe three or four people: the deputy editor, Simon Richardson, who offered me the job, and some colleagues who I'd met on the circuit in the Middle East before.

It was the summer, and I finally had the opportunity to report from the biggest annual sporting contest in the world, the Tour, and major cycling races across the UK, Europe, Asia and America.

I'd barely unpacked my suitcase before I had to repack it and leave for the continent, the Tour already underway. I arrived on either the first or second rest day. I can't remember which.

It had been raining incessantly in England but there wasn't a cloud in the sky in France and, walking across the tarmac, I'd closed my eyes momentarily to soak in the sun.

Later at a Team Sky press conference – the British squad, which would go on to win the first of many yellow jerseys – the same sun started to feel too intense. The media op with international press was hosted outside the squad's hotel and the only shade around was that shielding the riders perched behind a long rectangular table.

After the formal proceedings, everyone dispersed back into the hotel to do more informal interviews. Inside I found Australian cyclist Michael Rogers, who was riding for Sky at the time.

I sat next to him and fired away some questions about the race. I was meant to then move on and find someone else to talk to but instead I just sat there. I don't know if it was the effect of the sun or hearing another Australian accent or both, but I couldn't move.

Sacrificing the comforts of home to move to Europe and try to make something of yourself is an experience every Australian rider has had. And being so far away, sometimes you do feel isolated. It's not like after a bad couple of days you can pop back to see family or friends. It takes a weekend just to get home.

Rogers seemed to identify what was going on before I did. He started to tell me about his experiences when he moved to Italy as a rookie racer, not speaking a word of Italian and also knowing few people. It was rough. At least in the UK I could understand everyone, and they could understand me. For the most part.

It would get better, Rogers told me. And he was right. When

my UK visa expired in 2014, I initially didn't want to go back to Australia. There are riders who stay abroad after their racing careers have finished.

I had no expectations of what the Tour would be like because, unlike many, I didn't grow up watching it. One of my earliest memories is learning how to ride a bike and as a kid I cycled regularly to and from school and on weekends with my family. But I never thought about cycling as a professional sport until, as a rookie journalist working at the *Geelong Advertiser* in 2009, I was told cycling was going to be my new beat.

In 2010, I reported on the UCI Road World Championships, an annual event, which that year took place in Geelong and Melbourne, and ultimately became a springboard for my career.

I had watched the Tour only twice on TV before I became a part of it.

Once there I initially felt dazed, and the race was quite confronting, but over time, and with experience, I learned all the different unwritten rules journalists and riders are expected to abide by, and made friends, some of whom I now count among my best.

I am so focused while I am reporting during the Tour that, immediately after and before stages, I sometimes go into autopilot. While most international sports impose order and distance between athletes, journalists and fans, the Tour scene, before the onset of the COVID-19 pandemic, was often akin to the Wild West. Someone can be in my face saying hello and, unless it relates to whatever story or angle I am fixated on, I don't always register that they are even there.

The people who comprise the Tour – cyclists, team management and staff, media, officials and organisers – will often describe their general experience at the race as unparalleled stress, despite the inspiring stories that are written and broadcast. It's true the Tour takes it out of you in a way other events on the cycling calendar do not. Everyone begins the Tour looking sprightly but, even after a few days, appearances change. The crease marks of sleep deepen in people's cheeks, styled hairdos become unkempt, eyes start to droop and turn bloodshot.

If you stay in the race from the first stage to the last, you don't notice these changes until the end, but if you come in and out you do.

I admire colleagues who wake at 6 am or earlier to get a bit of exercise in before stages. Towards the end I am sleeping in as late as possible and nicking hotel coffee cups because I desperately need the caffeine hit but don't have enough time to sit in the restaurant.

And yet there is something about the Tour. The more you commit to it, the more it takes from you, but it's very addictive.

Usually, the Tour transcends global politics. It's a melting pot of cultures that offers an escape from the real world. The Tour changed dramatically in the first two years of the COVID-19 pandemic. In 2020 it was postponed from its usual June–July time slot to August–September, when people were still fearful of coronavirus, not fed up with lockdowns. I stayed in Australia that year and in the lead-up to the delayed race, which was by all accounts a smaller and quieter moving circus, wrote a column for *La Course En Tête*, questioning if it was responsible to move forward with it in the global climate. Not everyone agreed with that viewpoint.

In 2021, Australia had closed itself off from the rest of

the world and strongly discouraged its citizens from leaving, but after a long, expensive, and mostly maddening process I got government permission to exit the country on business. The Tour had returned to its usual time slot but wasn't at all what I knew. The TV compound normally full of hundreds of broadcast trucks was about a quarter of the size. So too was the press room. Face masks were required everywhere and, notably, journalists were segregated from teams by fences that ensured social distancing. Instead of bumping shoulders in the teams' paddock, you were confined to a designated area near the stage start or finish, shouting at a rider or sports director at a distance to stop. When, or if, they did, the conversation was all business. There was very little of what I would call human interaction. Road cycling is an international sport but still operates like a quintessential country town where everyone knows everyone.

Sometimes having a laugh with a sports director standing outside a team bus or walking alongside a rider who is slowly pedalling to the start line, and just asking how they are, a 60-second conversation, can tell you more about their condition, or what is happening in the race, than anything gleaned from a structured interview. The hardest thing about reporting on the 2020 Tour from Australia was that you missed out on the real stories, which are shared in those passing moments of light-hearted reprieve from an otherwise tense environment.

With the 2022 Grand Depart set to leave Copenhagen, Denmark, the future looks brighter for those of us who knew the race in all its messy glory before the pandemic.

One of my favourite memories from the Tour is the final stage of the 2019 edition. Weeks before we rolled into Paris, the capital had been divided by the yellow vests movement – which initially started due to anger over rising fuel prices in France but then grew broader and led to violence in the streets. You could still see what looked like empty tear gas canisters on the sides of the Champs-Élysées.

I was working for SBS television at the Tour that year and due to a conflict I tried to but could not resolve with the executive sports producer in France, it'd been a tough race. But then something happened that restored my faith in humanity.

A group of armed French national police officers were standing just up from the finish line. The media usually jumped the barricade onto the worn cobblestones to interview riders the moment the Tour was over. Technically, you weren't meant to unless you had certain accreditation. But with those guys there I didn't dare.

As the peloton completed the final laps of the Champs-Élysées one officer walked over to a massive group of colourful Colombian fans, who had turned out to see that year's Tour winner, Colombian Egan Bernal. The supporters didn't have hospitality tickets to sit front row, champagne and canapés in hand. They were much further back from the roadside, stood behind a barricade, their red, blue and yellow national flags catching the wind.

This officer reached into the crowd, picked up a boy who was recording the race with a phone and, holding the kid in his arms, walked back to the side of the road so the boy could film the action up close. The boy placed his small hand around the officer's neck to balance as he watched intently. Kindness replaced violence.

The Tour is more than a bike race sometimes. I've talked about it endlessly, written tens of thousands of words on it, done many TV crosses, radio segments, and still can't capture all the tales that make the race.

But here I hope to give you a behind-the-scenes taste of what the Tour is really like to be at, and a part of.

CHAPTER 1
FIRST IMPRESSIONS

The day after the Tour de France finishes nearly everyone who has competed in it will tell you they hate it. No, actually, they fucking hate it.

For some it's not even the day after it finishes, it's the day after the three-week race starts that they're questioning why they signed up.

And yet this feeling is at odds with the fact that those same people who say they hate the race will make personal and professional sacrifices, as well as physically, mentally and emotionally exhaust themselves, just to be selected.

The Tour is cycling's pinnacle event and financially underpins a sport that is wholly dependent on sponsorship, which usually comes in the form of rich benefactors. It takes place in July, the month before cycling's transfer window officially opens. Performances there can be the difference between a rider securing a contract for the next season, how many zeros are at the end of a deal, or even the fate of a team.

The top tier of competition in cycling is known as the WorldTour and currently there are thirty-three races that comprise the WorldTour calendar, including two other Grand Tours (the Giro d'Italia and the Vuelta a España). However, the Tour is popularly considered the only stage race that general sports fans, not just cycling nuts, know. It's an international spectacle. I have friends who, even when I was reporting on their TV screens, said they just tuned in for the scenery.

It has been a long time since one of Australia's best cyclists Richie Porte has watched the Tour and not been a protagonist in it, though he relates.

'Most people watch it for the scenery, let's be honest, because France is a beautiful country,' Porte says.

'It's chalk and cheese being in the race and watching it. It's two totally different things.

'When you watch the Tour on TV it looks like we're all riding along.' But even in the lulls, between the attacks and counterattacks, he adds, it's still stressful. It is a constant fight and there is a nervous energy in the peloton, especially at the beginning.

'Everyone wants to be at the front and there are only so many people who can be there,' Porte says.

What you see and read of the Tour belies some of the deeper, darker truths about the race and what people put themselves through – first just to get there, and then to compete. And I'm not talking about doping. It's a competition not only to win but just to survive.

Renowned sprinter Marcel Kittel, who won fourteen stages during his career, recalls the difference between viewing the

2

Tour as a kid growing up in Germany and competing between 2012 and 2018. During those years he became the benchmark of sprinting, but also had some of his most devastating days on the bike.

'For me the Tour without a doubt was in general the most important race of my career. It really defined my career, the success that I had there,' he says.

'When I did my first Tour de France in 2012, I didn't really know what to expect. It's a race that you only know from television, you hear so many things, and it really excites you as a young rider to think about your first start there.'

When it becomes a reality and riders experience the Tour firsthand their impression of the race changes.

'You don't see it through a camera lens,' Kittel continues, 'you're part of the stories that are told there and that's probably one of the things that surprised me most.

'In the end it's only a bike race and when you see the epic stories that are told around the race, it's not always what you feel as a rider because there are simply some days where you just do your job.

'Of course, it's hard but, what I want to say is, the media makes a big part of the story of the race and shapes its perception outside and I think you realise that once you are in it, as a rider especially.'

Only a tiny percentage of the infinite number of stories that compose the Tour are told. And as the saying goes, the stories that are often illustrated are the ones told by the winners, who predominately focus on their success, not what they endured to get it or the moments of insecurity and doubt they masked with bravado.

The truth is Tour competitors are fallible people, in competition with themselves as much as those they are pitted against. They can be certain one day and reduced to tears the next, seeking support from friends who can become enemies and enemies who can become friends in an environment where they are only as good as their last performance.

The Tour is one of the oldest races in cycling and considered the ultimate endurance test. The peloton, on average, cycles 3500 kilometres through France, and sometimes neighbouring nations, for twenty-one days, or twenty-one stages. The route changes every year, and each stage varies in length. The longest stage of the 2021 Tour was 249.1 km and Slovenian Matej Mohorič won it in just under five-and-a-half hours. German Roger Kluge was the last rider to officially finish that day and came in twenty-five minutes and three seconds behind Mohorič.

The race also typically includes two 'rest days' – one at the end of the first week and one at the end of the second. They are the only days the peloton isn't riding during the entire period of competition, but really there is no rest at the Tour. Those two days are filled with press conferences, and, for journalists, dashes to provincial laundromats.

There's no going home if you've had a bad day, no week between matches to compose yourself and try again. You do your best and fight through your worst, exposed to the elements and under the glare of the global spotlight.

There is a balance of different terrains – high mountain stages, medium mountain stages, rolling stages and flat stages. The overall journey is unpredictable and about the same length as a cross-country trek from Melbourne to Perth.

Add the distance spent travelling to stage starts, and leaving stage finishes for the next hotel, and you're looking at about a 5500-kilometre trip.

The race is composed of a myriad of components. There are usually around twenty-two teams consisting of eight riders – as well as sports directors, performance directors, managers, mechanics, doctors, chefs, coaches, drivers, massage therapists, *soigneurs*, communications and admin staff – each that take to the start line. The peloton competes for stage wins every day, and on top of that there are overarching competitions. The most renowned and prestigious of those is the fight for the yellow jersey, or *maillot jaune*. The time each rider takes to complete each stage is tallied over the entire Tour and listed on the 'general classification' or GC every day. The person who completes the Tour in the lowest cumulative time wins the yellow, or the race title. To be in contention for this you must be an all-rounder – able to climb the highest peaks, time trial, and stay safe at the front of the bunch or within shot of the front of the race at all times.

Most awards at the Tour are individual – only one person can win a stage, outside of team time trials; only one person can win the yellow jersey, the green jersey, the polka dot jersey, or the white jersey, given to the best young rider. But teamwork is crucial to that singular success.

Four-time champion Chris Froome had the support of the best team in business during his reign at the Tour. Cadel Evans believes his fight to win the yellow jersey was years-long because he couldn't count on the support of a strong squad before his 2011 conquest. Some pundits would say Slovenian prodigy Tadej Pogačar, who won the Tour in 2020 and 2021, is the exception to the rule, that he can win on his own, but rivals don't agree.

The Tour and road cycling in general is complex until you understand it. Then, it becomes enthralling. One of the things that makes it so interesting is that different stages suit different types of riders – sprinters, climbers, *puncheurs* (riders who can sprint but also climb over undulating terrain well), time trialists – and in every stage there are races within races, too. There will be the race to win the stage, and then, within that, moves and countermoves to gain time or points, which count towards winning overarching classifications.

As well as the fight for the yellow jersey, there are three other competitions suited to other types of riders. The 'points classification' is tailored to sprinters and *puncheurs*. There is a descending points scale at intermediate sprint primes along stage routes and at stage finishes. The biggest bonifications come from winning stages, and the rider with the most points at the end of the Tour wins the green jersey. Previous winners include Peter Sagan, Mark Cavendish, Sam Bennett, Erik Zabel, Tom Boonen and Australians Michael Matthews, Robbie McEwen and Baden Cook.

There is also the King of the Mountain (KOM) classification where the best climbers vie to win the red and white polka dot jersey. Points are awarded to the first riders who reach the top of designated 'KOM' summits on stages. The number of points awarded depends on the difficulty of each climb. The winner of the Tour and KOM is sometimes the same and sometimes different, depending how the race plays out. For example, a yellow jersey contender may not aim to be first over a KOM climb if it doesn't serve their bigger aim to win the race overall.

Froome won the polka dot jersey only once, but Pogačar has won it twice.

Finally, there is the Best Young Rider classification, which cyclists under the age of twenty-six can contest. Like the *maillot jaune* this prize is awarded to the rider with the lowest cumulative time. Past winners include Pogačar, who has claimed it along with the yellow and polka dot jersey from 2020–21, Egan Bernal, who won the white jersey the same year he claimed his first Tour title in 2019, as well as Adam and Simon Yates, Alberto Contador and Andy Schleck.

Every day at the Tour is full of action as cyclists compete for career-defining stage wins and, within those, available bonuses which contribute to their overall standings and chances of winning one of the jerseys, if they identify those as an objective.

Evans is the only Australian to have won the *maillot jaune*.

'How would I describe the Tour?' says Evans on the tenth anniversary of his win. 'If I had to say it in a word: stressful. Probably a more diplomatic term would be intense.

'A lot of people, they go in and maybe they're stage hunters or one-day riders and they find themselves in a good place, and maybe they find themselves in the leader's jersey of a Grand Tour and they're really just like, "How can you do this for twenty-one days?"

'They do it for one or two or three days and find themselves in a position that everything is so draining they can't deal with it.'

BikeExchange-Jayco head sports director Matt White believes that is what makes the Tour different. 'Everything around the Tour is amplified and more exciting, more stressful, however you look at it. It's just a bigger fishbowl than all of our other races.'

McEwen ventures that it is the timing of the Tour, held during the European summer holidays, that has made it an automatic winner.

'People are always shocked when they realise the enormity of the Tour de France. It's our grand slam, the one big one on the cycling calendar. Something has to be the biggest, and it just is,' McEwen says.

'And then from being the biggest, all the best riders want to be at the Tour and be there at their best.

'If it was said to me there is only one race you can ride in the season, you have to pick it, I'd go Tour.'

McEwen made his name at the race, winning twelve stages and three green jerseys during his career, so it's no surprise he'd commit to it above all else. But there were moments between his victories where he felt like he was being tortured. Moments where he would vomit because the pain was so terrible. Withdrawing from the race was never an option he, or anyone else for that matter, would willingly take.

'You try and get it done whatever the circumstances. And because I could actually still turn the pedals, I just kept turning the pedals,' he says.

It takes a special mentality to compete at the Tour. The competitors thrive off pain, not just there but during the season at large when they spend hundreds of days away from home training and racing.

'Everyone in this sport is making too [many] sacrifices not to enjoy it,' says White. Heinrich Haussler is the only rider I can think of who has said he hates the Tour de France and stayed away – albeit after winning a stage during his third participation in 2009. He returned twice afterwards, but the race didn't give him the same 'snot coming out my nose, spit hanging down my chin, mouth wide open breathing, fuck this is so hard' buzz that he later found in other disciplines, like cyclo-cross.

Usually, the relationship between the Tour and those who are part of it is less polarising. It's more like a love-hate kind of deal, as Belgian racer Jens Debusschere explains.

'Every year after the Tour, the first week after the Tour you say, "Next year, I don't want to do the Tour," or I will say immediately, "I don't want to go to the Tour." But once you restart in November, December, you're thinking about the Tour.'

If you include the week before the Tour officially starts with the Grand Depart, when everyone arrives for media preamble, sponsorship engagements and now COVID-19 testing, the Tour is one month on the road, working every day from the moment you wake up until when your head hits the pillow. No exaggeration.

It is another world, governed by different rules, and was referred to as a 'bubble' long before the word became part of the lexicon of the pandemic. You must buy into all of its parts – its virtue and ridiculousness – otherwise you won't last. I used to say the Tour was so encompassing that World War III could erupt and, unless it happened in front of me, I wouldn't know.

When you're in it, the Tour, everything else fades away.

CHAPTER 2
GRAND DEPART

For many the journey to the Tour de France begins from childhood.

Three-time stage winner and 2017 green jersey champion Michael Matthews recalls being awestruck watching it as a kid growing up half a world away in Canberra.

'From when I first started cycling, I was not really even into cycling, but I was doing it just out of enjoyment of the sport, didn't know too much about the history,' he says.

'We would always, with my group of cycling friends, stay up and watch the Tour de France and think how the guys were superstars.

'And to now think that I've ridden that same race that those guys were in is pretty special.'

Tour competitors claim they don't think about the race until it's upon them in June and July each year. The Tour falls around the middle of a nine-month road season that runs from January through to October and the riders have other objectives in the lead-up to the Tour, from competing in one-day races, like the spring classics, to new as well as established week-long stage races across the globe.

Irish sprinter Sam Bennett and Matthews are among those who say they prefer not to think about the Tour until they must, instead focusing on other big objectives that come before it.

Matthews's first goal of the season is traditionally the Ardennes Classics, and his training and dialogue revolves around that, not the Tour where he is also expected to perform.

'There are so many races leading up to it that are also very important for me,' says Matthews.

'The Tour de France, once you get there, it's such a big stress ball, a circus, you have enough stress when you get there, so thinking about it for the months leading up to it is a waste of energy, to be honest. I try and zone out from it and then once we get to the start line then that's where it starts to get a bit more real.'

The thing is, all those objectives along the way count towards the Tour. It's the one race that I refer to in interviews year-round and teams plan endlessly for.

Every marquee pure sprinter, like Bennett, typically competes at the UAE Tour in February. It is contested in front of a handful of invited media, some sheiks, a spattering of expats and, the closer you get to the border of Oman, with its sheer, brown rock mountains, the odd goat.

It's nothing like the Tour but a winning campaign in the desert creates momentum that can set the tone all the way up to, and including, the big one in July.

'During the season, the Tour de France seems to be the place where people judge sprinters,' says Bennett, 'and now it's kind of becoming that UAE is the early season race that people judge the sprinters [by] as well because everybody is there, most of the guys are there.

'It's nice to have a good run of results there.'

Preparation for the Tour de France begins as early as October the year before when the route for the season ahead is revealed in Paris. That's generally when team managers and sports directors start to make broad stroke plans, including rider selection based firstly on course suitability.

Managers outline Grand Tour squads on the eve of new seasons now, and it's common for riders in each of those to share the same race program in the lead-up, so that they learn to work soundly together.

A few months out from the Grand Depart, the Tour then comes sharply into focus and training is ramped up. In the lead-up to the 2021 edition Richie Porte was clocking 42-hour weeks on the bike during an Ineos Grenadiers team training camp.

Around this time, teams reconnoitre specific stages either in person or via videos available on YouTube. They are on regimented diets and participate in further high-altitude training camps.

At the start of the 2021 season virtually everyone I interviewed was at altitude, atop a dormant volcano or imposing mountain.

Matt White was with his BikeExchange team in Sierra Nevada in Spain. At the base of the mountain it was 22 degrees Celsius. Where he was it was minus 8 degrees.

'We're really high,' White remarked via a patchy line. 'It's good skiing, people out skiing out the window.'

Matthews, who rides for BikeExchange–Jayco, was succinct

in his summation of the camp's difficulty when he was driving home from it, his *soigneur* at the wheel: 'I'm pretty fucked at the moment, but I'm sure, give me a couple of days and I'll be better again. We just trained full gas for three weeks. It was [a] pretty heavy training camp.'

In the immediate lead-up to the Grand Depart, which the first stage of the Tour is always referred to as, it's all about organisation, logistics and packing.

Team chefs are loading their kitchen trucks which they work out of during the race with dry goods and speciality ingredients. Journalists arrive at whatever city in whatever country the race commences to collect accreditation and the road book. The rood book at the Tour is akin to a bible. They are printed in French and in English and issued sparingly – one per person. I write my name on the front cover the second I get it and am reluctant to hand it over to someone who asks to borrow it thereafter, in case they lose it.

The road book is a stage-by-stage breakdown of the race and includes important information about each route and rest day. This incorporates stage profiles, maps of approaches at the start and finishes and information on how to access them, a kilometre-by-kilometre breakdown of stages as well as anticipated start and finish times going on three different average speeds the peloton may travel at – fastest, moderate, slowest – plus a load of facts about every city, village and town that hosts a stage. There's a list of teams competing, contact information, details on prize money. Prior to the pandemic the road book used to list team hotel locations too. But in 2021 they were omitted, and the quality of paper was noticeably cheaper too. The official reason for this was a publicised focus

14

on recycling, which organisers have before placed an emphasis on, reducing where riders can litter, that is, discard empty *bidons*, or drink bottles, and food wrappers along the route. Then there are the portable hay toilet cubicles in the TV compound. Some poor person has to fill up biodegradable plastic bags with hay and place them in what are effectively drop toilets. They leave a spade and extra hay beside every loo. Once you've done your business, you cover it with hay and leave it for the next person. I'm all for saving the planet, minimising global warming and helping the animals, but I cannot articulate how wretched these things smell at the end of a 35-degree-plus day, even after they're cleaned regularly.

The men can use outdoor plastic urinals. Us women aren't so lucky unless we can locate a Portaloo with a flush, or the press room, from which written media work, and which has proper facilities.

Race organiser ASO say recycling, I say budget cuts.

The Tour de France always begins differently. Unlike the finish in Paris, which is a mainstay, where the race kicks off changes annually. From its first running in 1903 to 1953 it was hosted exclusively inside France but then ventured outside the nation, to the Netherlands and Belgium, what was known as West Germany in 1965, Switzerland in 1982, Spain in 1992, Ireland in 1998 and beyond. In my time it has commenced in Wallonia, Belgium, Corsica, in France, Yorkshire, England, which has developed legend status, riders and sports directors still refer to it today, the university town of Utrecht in the Netherlands, other areas of France and Germany.

Former Paris-Roubaix winner Mathew Hayman was 'over the moon' when he made his Tour de France debut as an experienced veteran in Yorkshire. He still remembers it vividly.

'Yorkshire in the UK, the crowds were just next level. I'd never been in a race anything like that,' he says.

My UK visa expired prior to the Yorkshire Grand Depart and I had to move to Spain before rejoining the race in France. I was gutted, not just because I'd heard how great it was, and seen pictures from the start where there wasn't a visible patch of concrete amid the throng of supporters on every roadside and vantage point, but because the Duke and Duchess of Cambridge plus Prince Harry were in town and part of the podium ceremony at the end of the first stage.

There is a daily podium ceremony at the Tour where the stage winner and jersey leaders are presented. In years gone by immaculately dressed podium girls hand them flowers, trophies and then, standing either side of the cyclist being accoladed, kiss their cheeks as they pose for a celebratory photo.

Marcel Kittel recalls winning the first stage in Yorkshire to meet the future of the British monarchy in what was a unique presentation.

'Before I went up to the podium, I was also instructed, "Don't give kisses to Kate, just shake hands, be polite, they are royals, so, yeah, show some respect,"' he says.

'I think I was way more impressed by them than they were by me, but it was a great experience and very nice podium picture that now I have with the royal family.'

The Grand Depart varies in terrain every season too. Sometimes it is a flat stage for the pure sprinters, who when vying for line honours generally contest what's called a bunch sprint, when the peloton arrives at the finish line all together.

It provides them with a rare opportunity to wear the yellow leader's jersey for a stint at the beginning of the race. Other times it has been a prologue, a short time trial between roughly five to nine kilometres long, or a longer time trial. There are lumpier stages suited to the *puncheurs*. Generally, the real yellow jersey contenders must wait for their chances, which come later in the piece.

The Grand Departs I have reported on from the ground are a bit of a blur. To be honest, I remember them for the food, ambience and cultural experience. When the Tour started in Brussels in 2019, you bet I ordered a Belgian staple dish, *moules-frites* (mussels and French fries) at least once.

At every start line there are stands containing bottled water, bananas and a vast supply of different flavoured energy gels and bars, which riders will pick at and stuff in their back pockets before they set off for another day of racing.

There's also the Tour Village, filled with VIP suites, merchandise stores and stalls laden with drinks and snacks for accredited patrons.

The bonus of the Grand Depart is that the second and third stage are normally hosted in and around the same region. So, if you're lucky you'll stay in the same hotel for multiple nights and be able to socialise with colleagues, provided everyone is staying close by, but that's usually not the case. I think the last big dinner I was at was Utrecht in 2015.

One of the most vivid Grand Departs was in Corsica in 2013. The mountainous, Mediterranean island is a territory of France, southeast of the mainland, but going on the architecture you could have been forgiven for thinking you were in Italy, which the place has historical ties to. Different again is the flag of Corsica, a black and white design featuring a Moor's head. I'd never seen it before.

So much is at stake during the Tour that, in the first week especially and crashes are almost inevitable. Corsica was no exception.

It all started when the Orica–GreenEDGE team bus got stuck under the gantry at the finish line in Bastia as the peloton prepared for a bunch sprint with about 12 kilometres remaining.

Cameron Meyer made his Tour debut with the team at that edition of the race.

'The first week of that Tour was very eventful,' he recalls.

In short, race officials decided to move the finish line up to the three-kilometre to go mark in lieu of the bus that was wedged tight. That was communicated to all teams over the crackling race radio.

But then, the bus managed to get clear, and the finish line was restored to its original place.

Kittel navigated the confusion and then crash carnage to win his maiden Tour stage in what was his second race appearance.

'When we came into that final, everything went well and then this whole chaos started to begin, with these weird commands and communication on our radio, when they suddenly said, "the finish is not at the finish line."'

Kittel continues, 'A few minutes later they said the finish is again at the finish line because of this bus that got stuck.

'I took my earpiece out and thought, "Okay that's really weird." I just tried to focus on my sprint and do my best.

'Once we left this narrow section hell broke loose. There was this massive crash where [compatriot] Tony Martin lost a lot of skin, but we could pull through as a team to the finish and we also took the lead in the final and really tried to make the race and shape our own luck and success there.'

Martin reportedly lost consciousness twice after the stage following his crash. He was later cleared of fractures but suffered from a concussion, lung contusion, soft tissue damage over his body, and a deep, five-centimetre wound on his left elbow.

But he went on to win a stage with a rival team and finish the Tour.

At the finish there was so much happening that I went into autopilot and can't recall it all vividly. It became a bit like a water painting, clear but blurry at the same time.

The two medium mountain stages that followed were almost as large, with Orica–GreenEDGE redeeming its bus faux pas. Simon Gerrans won stage three, the team's first ever victory at the Tour, and then the squad, back on the mainland the next day, claimed the team time trial.

'We took the yellow jersey for four days where we had it with Gerrans and it swapped to Daryl Impey,' Meyer recalls.

'It was crazy good for Australian cycling to have an Australian team, the public really got behind us and saw us winning on the biggest stage, so I have really fond memories of the Tour.

'When I watch it on TV, I cringe a little bit because it is one of the hardest bike races in the world, it's got its dangers to it, it's got its crashes but for me it was a memorable experience.'

After the first week, Jens Debusschere says, the Tour peloton is less nervous, and so generally there are fewer crashes.

'You have your spot in the bunch and you know which stages

19

you're there for, and which stages you need to be at your highest level, which stages you can do – well, never easy, but you can handle easy,' he says.

'So, then everything calms down a little bit. And, after the first week, you know your level, like, I'm suffering every day, or I'm quite comfortable in the bunch and I can let go on that climb without any trouble of being out of [the] time cut.'

There are no substitutions during the Tour. You can't sit out a couple of stages if you feel rough and then get back into it. If you don't start a stage, you're out of the race, and if you don't finish a stage within the time cut you are also gone.

Time cuts at the Tour are designed to stop people taking hours to finish a stage. Simplified, they are calculated as a percentage of the stage winner's time but also at the discretion of officials.

On a short mountain stage of the 2018 Tour that Geraint Thomas won, a number of sprinters, including Kittel and Mark Cavendish, both finished but missed the cut and were eliminated from the Tour.

Sprinters and *puncheurs*, classics specialists, on mountain stages have to work particularly hard to make the time cut as the sinewy climbers and title contenders, physically suited to the ascents, duel for victory at the front of the race.

The riders who must fight against the clock on these days form what's called a *grupetto*. The *grupetto* is generally the last big group on the road and those within it temporarily put rivalry aside to work together and reach the finish in time.

'The Tour de France is a bit different to the Giro. They've all got their own rules about how far behind the peloton, or the winner, you're allowed to finish, and the Tour has some very tight time cuts and that causes a lot of anxiety in the group, especially guys that can't climb very well,' says Hayman.

'You have to be able to be there and you can't lose the wheel.

'Everybody wants to be in front of the *grupetto* and have that safety net behind them, to know there's forty guys coming behind and that's your safety net. But when everybody does that – and we're talking about the world's best – and everybody wants to just be in front of the group of guys that are struggling, it's pretty hard to be in front of the struggling guys!'

Hayman continues, 'It's a race too, and normally there's some older guys that just say, "Enough is enough, we're comfortable," and they've got the experience to say, "Look, we're only this far down and we're going to be alright today," and they'll generally set a pace on the climb that they know, you're going to lose x amount of minutes per kilometre and you'll be fine.'

When the peloton reaches the finish line each day, journalists were before the pandemic able to sprint up to and run alongside them to wherever they stopped, whether it was just over the line, further down the road or at the team bus.

So close, you could see white salt stains on their jerseys from where they had perspired; hear them cough and rapidly gasp for breath, issue a guttural roar in celebration or swear in aggrievance; watch them scull a soft drink after a hot day, or see their lips turn blue and their teeth chatter on a mountain pass. On some days, they'd recover quickly enough to laugh with you.

The heaving press pack moved like a rugby maul, governed only by unwritten rules that did not dissuade the complete violation of personal space or the odd hip and shoulder. I can't imagine another workplace where grown adults chasing each other is an acceptable practice.

I was also not above the argy bargy that sometimes emanated from the pack. On a cold day one year in the Pyrenees, I was stood in a group huddled around Tom Dumoulin, who is ever patient and answers interviews in his native Dutch and then English. I started to feel dizzy as he went to begin the English round. There's something about the Pyrenees, every time I'm there I feel like I'm suffering from vertigo.

I could hear someone rushing up behind me, then they yanked my ponytail, I assume to try and better position themselves. I sharply threw my elbow back and it connected with their ribs.

The next minute, I felt the lens of a heavy TV camera resting on my head, but that guy turned out to be my guy, who was struggling to get a clear shot above all the clambering heads.

During the Tour, I run on the adrenaline that is tangible in the air.

I've reported from nine editions of the race since my first in 2012.

I missed the 2020 edition, but after running the gauntlet to get back there in 2021, my perception of the race drastically changed. For the first time, real world events pierced the bubble I operated within there. The Tour has only ever stopped for the two World Wars.

Race organiser ASO and other parties found a way to navigate through COVID-19. However, the pandemic altered the face of the Tour. Outside of the actual racing, the day-to-day processes around that became a much more ordered affair. There was a literal and metaphorical distance now between those competing and those reporting on and engaging in the race, in line with most other international sports.

Some riders enjoyed not being so close to the masses. Bennett reasoned the segregation was not as sociable, but was effectively more normal, if not professional. Media and fans had their designated spaces, and the riders didn't have to negotiate human traffic when moving to and from team buses at stage starts and finishes.

'It just seems to be a more organised way of getting to people than before when we just used to meet at random points on the road, or beside the bus or something,' says Bennett.

I hated it. I was at the Tour but felt unable to get my finger on its pulse like normal, and that's what stimulates and sustains the adrenaline, which, as fatigue starts, prevents you from collapsing.

Earlier in the season I had interviewed Cherie Pridham after she became the first female sports director to work in the WorldTour.

She had signed with the Israel Start-Up Nation team, directing the likes of Chris Froome as well as Dan Martin and Michael Woods. I'd asked her what the biggest challenge of her new appointment had been so far, expecting her to say something about being a woman in a man's world, which I'm familiar with.

We got to that: Pridham later reflected how some fans still appear surprised when they see a woman behind the wheel as the team cars roll out in a convoy behind the peloton and follow it at races. 'Especially when you're driving through starts and you can hear, you sort of hover next to a crowd or something and you hear, "Oh, there's a woman in there."

'Yeah, and?' Pridham says.

But that wasn't her first answer.

'The fact that we're dealing with a pandemic, getting to races. I mean, I still consider us privileged and extremely lucky to be able to carry on with our job to a certain degree,' she says. 'But, you know, just to get on a plane now you need a suitcase of paperwork, and it takes a week to get that paperwork together just to be able to travel.'

At the time I didn't appreciate the observation but come the 2021 Tour I understood. After I'd managed to leave Australia, the government changed the quarantine hotel caps and I faced the prospect of being indefinitely stranded in Europe when my return flight was cancelled as a result.

But when questioned if I'd do it all again, the answer was simple. Yes.

As every rider knows, there is a price you pay for the privilege of competing at the Tour de France.

CHAPTER 3
HUNGER PAINS

The Tour de France peloton appears emaciated when it lines up at the Grand Depart. The supple, sun-kissed skin of title contenders is stretched tight across overexposed cheekbones. They walk gingerly on bowed legs resembling those of an old man at the end of his life, not one in his prime able to climb thousands of metres above sea level.

Sprinters who can hit around 70 kilometres an hour when vying for a stage win have brawny quads and toned, bubble-butt backsides but are still lithe, their protruded collarbones hidden under lightweight team jerseys. Climbers sport biceps the size of a slender woman's wrist, and pale, hollowed chests that don't see the sun.

The riders' pronounced tan lines, from sunglasses and helmet straps, give a superficial indication as to how much training they have done, how 'ready' they are.

So, too, does their weight.

Weight, and power-to-weight ratio, is perceived as a key performance gain in cycling.

The general appearance of the riders is at odds with the fact that they consume and burn between an estimated 6000 to 9000 calories a day during the three-week marathon. The top end of that scale is the equivalent of about seven large Big Mac meals, and is more than three times greater than the recommended daily calorie intake of the average male. To consume the immense number of calories they need to compete, Tour riders eat around seven chef-prepared dishes a day, from breakfast through to a late supper. But mealtime at the Tour is not a gastronomic experience: it's a chore.

The specifics of it are fascinating but at first glance not appetising. Just opening a bain-marie full of plain spiral pasta at 7 am makes me baulk, let alone stomaching it.

How chefs approach their job now, the boundaries they must work within, is different to that of their predecessors.

Matt White recalls, 'My last Grand Tour in 2007, the Giro d'Italia, we had a chef, but the chef was serving us red meat and pasta for twenty-one days in a row for dinner.

'The chefs then were there more to guarantee the quality of the food, not so much what we were eating. Whereas now the chefs and nutritionists, it's about what you're eating at certain times. There's a lot more science gone into that side. It had started then, but it's developed a hell of a long way in fifteen years.'

White believes that development as well as more specific and structured training helps explain the immediate and high-profile success of younger riders now, like Egan Bernal winning the yellow jersey at twenty-two and Tadej Pogačar at twenty-one.

'I think that's the reason why you're seeing these young guys ticking boxes very early because a lot of them are starting that professionalism with nutrition and training at a lot younger age,' White says.

You could equally argue that this focus on nutrition has contributed to the success of Ineos Grenadiers and its former incarnation as Team Sky, which coined the phrase 'marginal gains' – making small changes which accumulate to larger improvements.

British chef James Forsyth had to forget everything he learned working in fine dining restaurants like Dinner by Heston Blumenthal upon joining the team.

Decadence was once Forsyth's remit but since his appointment it has become functionality over flavour.

He is one of three chefs employed at Ineos Grenadiers but is singlehandedly responsible for feeding the Tour squad, which from 2012 to 2019 won seven yellow jerseys with four different riders – Bradley Wiggins, Chris Froome, Geraint Thomas and Bernal.

'With it being known as one of the best cycling teams, there is always that pressure of having to produce something which is the best also,' he says.

You wouldn't think the intricacies between creating a component of Blumenthal's famous Meat Fruit and loading the most recognisable Tour de France competitors with pasta and rice would be much the same, but they are.

The boundaries in which Forsyth works are incredibly strict.

'Every ingredient has to have a purpose, so sometimes you do have to sacrifice how good something could be for it to be as nutritionally beneficial as possible,' he says. 'We could be making something which if I was working in a restaurant, I know it would need a few tablespoons of butter to make it perfect. But we have to bypass that and figure out something else, or just leave it out completely.'

Forsyth doesn't mention red meat. It's always white meat – chicken or fish. He hardly refers to dairy and uses coconut oil as a substitute for olive or vegetable oil.

'We're really, really minimal on cheese, you know, just a little bit of parmesan on the pasta is allowed,' he says. 'We'll fry a pancake in a little bit of coconut oil, or we'll put a little bit in the porridge to give a few extra calories before a big stage but that's about it.'

One of the challenges of Forsyth's job is to add colour to the black-and-white meal plans team nutritionists formulate, creating dishes that riders will be encouraged to eat.

'You want to try and move away from the plain pasta, the plain chicken and jazz it up, make it something special for them, as well as being healthy. There is always that pressure of wanting to impress, but obviously keep it within the boundaries of what is accepted.'

During the Tour, Forsyth himself runs off chocolate and energy drinks but I imagine that, like the beers team bus drivers apparently procure for evening knockoffs, the chocolate is hidden from the riders.

'Week three the biggest request is probably chocolate,' says Forsyth, 'you know, Nutella on the table or some sort of guilty dessert, a tiramisu or something.

'They can ask for it but they're not going to get it.

'When it comes to a Grand Tour the riders tend to accept that they need to keep it basic and stick to the nutrition plan, eat that four hundred grams of rice or whatever it is for breakfast.'

The plat du jour during Robbie McEwen's Tour career also consisted of protein and carbs, but mealtime was less scientific or governed than now. He was allowed chocolate.

'We had team chefs and generally that was about having good, clean healthy food but also eating stuff that you liked, and it was appetising. Especially when you're a couple of weeks into a Grand Tour, you get a bit over it,' McEwen says.

'I'd get to a certain day and say, "Hey, chef, if you're going to the markets and you find a nice tuna steak grab one for me." That's really good, high-quality protein. But I also liked to go back to my room and have a bar of chocolate, or a block of chocolate!

'I would have my cereal and whatever else. If it was a really long stage, some rice or a bit of pasta but I'd also always have Nutella on my toast.'

Every year Forsyth begins to prepare for the Tour a few months before the Grand Depart. A week out from the start, he will get the kitchen truck cleaned and packed before leaving for the race. Since the onset of the COVID-19 pandemic, Forsyth has worked out of the truck as opposed to taking over hotel kitchens.

Unlike his experience in restaurants, where four or five chefs may contribute a component to a single dish, Forsyth says the biggest pressure during the Tour is that everything is on him.

'It's a hell of a workload,' he says. 'We do have a driver for the kitchen truck, who helps out with the dishes and setting up at the restaurant, but the food is solely my responsibility.

'If you do not prepare something properly that's safe to eat, then it has massive consequences.'

That is something Michael Matthews is familiar with, and one which after the 2018 Tour altered his palate permanently.

Matthews was competing with Sunweb that year as the defending green jersey champion and recalls having had dinner later than usual after doing loads of interviews the evening of stage 4. He was one of the favourites for stage 5.

'I had white fish and I haven't had it since. I'm mentally scarred from white fish now,' Matthews says.

'I woke up exactly eight hours after [dinner], which is normally food poisoning, six to eight hours after you get the stomach problems. I woke up at three in the morning with a massive fever, sweating like crazy and vomiting [up] everything that was in my stomach. I remember doing that for about an hour.'

Matthews didn't improve as sunrise beckoned but summoned the strength to get out of bed for breakfast.

'The team tried to give me liquid meals but in the end that also just made me vomit.'

Despite his best efforts, Matthews was forced to abandon before the start of stage 5.

'The really sad thing was that afternoon, after I had rest and a lot of fluid, I was actually totally fine again, but obviously the stage has started,' he says.

'It was definitely hard to accept that Tour de France, where it just wasn't possible to continue.'

As Forsyth notes, for the chef, 'There is that pressure of making sure that everything is on point, every single mealtime.'

Forsyth's work on-site commences with cooking breakfast, lunch, and dinner four to five days out from the Grand Depart when everyone arrives.

'That first week before the start of the race is the busiest week of the whole Tour,' Forsyth says. 'You're cooking extra meals and there's a lot of extra planning and talks going on in that week as well.'

Once the Tour starts, on a normal day, Forsyth will wake up at 6 am, be in the kitchen truck working from 6.30 am and then it is nonstop until he clocks off around 11 pm.

Breakfast is a high-carb meal. There will be rice and pasta. But then he does eggs cooked to order – poached, fried or omelette – and three different types of porridge.

'It'll be a hot porridge, an overnight oats, soaked with milk and yoghurt and some apple and fruits, and we'll do a baked oat dish as well,' he says. 'And then we'll supplement that with cured meats and some salmon, fresh berries and a couple of different purees as well, maybe like an apple and vanilla puree and a banana yoghurt puree, just for a bit of extra micronutrients and fibre.'

After the Grenadiers have eaten breakfast and boarded the team bus to travel to that day's stage start, Forsyth packs up the kitchen truck and does a grocery shop himself at the local supermarket.

Then he sets up to prepare dinner at the next hotel, which is usually within thirty minutes to an hour of wherever the stage finishes.

'Evening time, again, it's just carbs everywhere,' he says. 'We do a couple of different rice dishes, so one plain and we'll do a flavoured one as well for the guys who like it a little bit more jazzy, a risotto, or a stir-fry rice.'

Forsyth will make a pasta dish in the evenings with sauce fresh to order.

'We do two proteins in the evening, so one meat and one fish dish, and a couple of vegetable dishes as well normally,' he continues.

'We try and keep a green vegetable dish every night, or a mixture of greens, and then one whether it's a salad, like a raw salad, or even a roasted vegetable dish.'

There is also, despite Forsyth's disregard for Nutella, dessert.

'And then dessert, it will depend on the next day's stage,' he continues. 'If it's just a flat day, we'll just do a simple fruit salad. But for the ones that they have to really fuel up for, we'll do maybe like a rice pudding or some sort of carb-based dessert as well for the bigger days.'

He's found that it's the simple things that keep the riders going, especially during the third week when the finish is so close but still so far and you must fight to prevent your body from automatically shutting down. Burger night has become a tradition for Ineos Grenadiers at the end of the penultimate stage when functionality finally gives way.

'That's something that keeps them going in the last week!' Forsyth says.

'You always drop into conversation, "Just think of the burger in a few days' time."'

Needless to ask if they'd like fries with that.

* * *

Food plays a big role in cycling and, more importantly, riders are commonly objectified over what they tip the scales at.

The entire industry is guilty of leering at competitors. This happens especially at early season races, like the Tour Down Under, when a rider's physique is callously judged in whispers and sideways glances on a scale of 'Watch out!' to 'That fat fuck has no chance of winning the Tour de France.'

In a feature I wrote for *Procycling* magazine about mental health and wellbeing in the peloton, Richie Porte illustrated what it felt like to be at the receiving end.

'If you turn up to race [in Europe] a couple of kilograms over what you were in Tour Down Under, the amount of riders that say stuff to you is ...' he trailed off.

'In the modern world you don't get away with commenting on that [weight], but you have riders and staff who think it's their right to.'

Porte, who finished third overall at the 2020 Tour in what was Australia's second-best performance on general classification in the history of the race, is resigned to it.

'When you see some of the food you can't eat, and you're burning so many thousands of calories per day and then you're having to be strict on the diet, it's not easy. But that's just one of the sacrifices you have to make,' he says. 'You're in a sport where power-to-weight is a huge factor. That's how it is.'

The process of preparing for the Tour – from rigorous diets and meal plans to training camps and hundreds of days away on the road – was one of the reasons Mathew Hayman decided to retire in 2019 after competing in cycling's top tier for almost two decades.

'You do get judged on it,' Hayman says. 'You turn up to a race and the mechanics, the *soigneur*, the directors, everybody looks you straight up and down and goes, "Okay, he's in okay shape." And that might have nothing to do with form, it's just your weight. It's just kind of accepted. It's a pretty harsh reality though.

'There's no real getting around it. It's physics.'

Today Hayman is two kilograms lighter than what he was as a racer, and it pisses him off.

'It took me years to try and lose a kilo and now I'm not racing anymore and I'm lighter!' he exclaims.

Hayman can joke about it now but during his racing career mealtime wasn't a laughing matter, even when he lined up at the Tour for the first time as an experienced thirty-six-year-old veteran.

He'd waited just shy of a decade to make his debut at the Tour in 2014. During stage 10, on the way to La Planche des Belles Filles, in the Vosges Mountains, visibility was so bad he had to ride behind a team car from which his sports director, using a GPS, would point left or right, so Hayman knew which way to turn.

'It was constant five-to-six-kilometre climbs all day – just up and down, up and down – it wasn't two massive climbs or anything, it just didn't stop,' Hayman recalls.

He missed a corner and crashed but got up and kept going, alone in the misty rain. Then he started hearing time checks through the race radio, and something about the finish on the hill before he felt his cleats instantaneously unlock from the pedals.

'Next minute I just clicked out,' Hayman recalls.

'I clicked out and it was almost like, as soon as I did, I remember getting in the car and then it was you can't turn it back. It's done.

'I pretty much broke down and nobody knew what to say.

These two guys [in the team car] had just watched me die for the last four and a half hours, they were in silence, they know what it means to you and there's not much you can say to somebody.'

It was a moment he now puts down to diet and performance anxiety. 'In hindsight [I] probably overdid the training on the way in and spent some extra time at altitude and was trying to drop too much weight.'

Two years later he went on to win the prestigious Paris–Roubaix cobblestone classic.

When I ask Hayman if eating became a labour during his racing career the tall and lanky Australian recalls his former relationship with food and stops just short of saying he had an eating disorder.

'I'm sure at some stages I've come close to … you know,' Hayman pauses. And then sighs.

'Well, you know, I guess it's an eating disorder if it's all-consuming. And it's never been so all-consuming that I've totally lost control, but it's something that's pretty forefront of every day, what you're putting into your mouth, and you're judging yourself every time you eat on whether you need it. That's not a particularly nice way to live.'

He admits it became obsessive.

'You are training that much that you are constantly hungry and you never kind of feel satisfied. You're constantly making choices,' he says.

Those choices are sometimes visible to others. Years ago, when I was living briefly in the cycling mecca of Girona, Spain, I went out to dinner with a bunch of cyclists who are based in the medieval village during the season. In the restaurant at one end of the table was a group of neo-pros – second and maybe even some third-year riders. At my end were the seasoned warhorses. The young guys approached their plates like hungry labrador puppies, laughing together as they hunched over and enthusiastically shovelled food in. At the other end of the table you could almost see the older riders calorie-counting in their heads. If they had one more glass of red wine, they couldn't have a dessert. Or, if they had dessert, they couldn't have another glass of wine.

Hayman wasn't at the table that night but analysing everything he consumed was a daily habit.

'I remember as a rider it was like, "Okay, how far is it to the airport? How long is that flight going to be? How far until we get to the next hotel? When is lunch going to be?"' he recalls. 'You really can't just miss a meal for a few hours, your body is constantly burning through energy and you're constantly feeling hungry.

'It was a constant kind of battle, too, to say, "I shouldn't be eating this but I'm kind of hungry. Am I really hungry? Am I not really hungry? What is my weight? How far until the Tour? Does it really matter?"'

In retirement, Hayman doesn't constantly think about food as he did throughout his Tour career. 'My life doesn't revolve around food now, is what I say. I don't count how many hours until my next meal.'

I've heard stories of Tour competitors who have tried to survive for a day, or even days, on tubs of yoghurt.

One year at the Tour I watched as the TV cameras caught Tejay van Garderen climbing off his bike during a stage. Van Garderen was long touted as 'America's next Tour winner' and was doing well. So, when he stopped on the roadside, shoulders dropped, face twisted in child-like despair, appearing as if there wasn't a sniff of energy left in his weakened body, which he could barely hold up, it was heart-wrenching. Days later a sports director mentioned that van Garderen hadn't eaten enough.

Performance nutritionist Martijn Redegeld, who works for Team Jumbo–Visma, has seen it all and believes that what riders consume – or don't consume – is the difference between winning and losing at the Tour.

'There is an old way of thinking that the day before the race guys need to eat, I don't know, maybe five or six or seven thousand calories because the next day will be a super hard day. In the past we have seen when the guys did that … the morning of the race they were one or two kilos heavier than the day before.'

Jumbo–Visma has become one of the pre-eminent teams in the WorldTour and it's fair to argue its work behind the scenes is testament to that.

The squad has developed an app called the Jumbo Food Coach, which provides individual, tailored meal plans to every rider. When they open the app riders are told what to eat, how much and when.

Redegeld believes that a bad day at the Tour, outside of a crash or injury, can be attributed to nutrition.

'A lot of guys when they do such hard races over two or three weeks, they cannot trust their own feeling anymore. So, they're not able to tell you anymore if they are hungry or if they are not hungry,' he says.

'What we have seen often is when that happens some guys are prone to eating too little so they lose weight, they don't have enough energy anymore in the body and you see that sometimes in the Grand Tours – when one of the favourite riders suddenly has a complete day off, that's most of the time not because he has lost his form, or because he doesn't have the right shape anymore but, I think almost in all the cases, he just didn't have enough fuel after the day before.'

Working at the Tour near riders and looking at their frames over the years I've wondered what the line is between performance-ready and anorexia or eating disorder.

However, Redegeld says it's more common for riders to eat too much rather than not enough.

'When they cannot really trust their own feeling anymore, they start eating too much,' he continues. 'They are afraid they have too little energy and they're like, "Okay, I take an extra scoop of rice, I take an extra slice of bread," or whatever, and in the end they have enough fuel in the body, but you see also that the body weight can increase one, two or sometimes even more kilograms during a three-week race, and by the end of the two or three weeks that can make a huge difference.'

One of the benefits of the Jumbo–Visma food app is that riders don't have to trust their own feelings or question whether they have had too much or enough.

Jumbo–Visma's philosophy is to bring its riders into 'energy balance', which is to ensure they consume the same number of calories that they burn. That varies for every rider, so each meal is different. Rider A may get 400 grams of rice and 100 grams of chicken and Rider B may get 300 grams of rice and 200 grams of chicken, or whatever it is.

In calculating that, Redegeld refers to not just performance data but the role of riders during a specific stage, team tactics and even the weather.

'I start analysing every stage, together with our trainers, and make a prediction: what are the needs and the nutritional needs for the riders in every stage and basically in every meal,' he says.

'Then, when we look into the timing of the different meals, we try to have them [eat] seven meals a day, so that's basically the breakfast, a little snack in the bus before they start the race, then of course they eat and drink on the bike, and then by the time they finish they have already two recovery meals in the bus on the way to the hotel.

'And then in the hotel, they have their dinner and then before they go to bed, they have also a late-night snack.'

The number and timing of the meals makes it easier for riders to consume the calories they need, compared to stomaching two or three huge, carb-loaded dishes.

'In the recovery phase it's really important that they have a few smaller meals because that's more beneficial for the recovery compared to everything together in one meal,' Redegeld says.

'Now the guys notice they can still start the race with the same amount of fuel or energy, but the weight is the same or sometimes even a little bit less than the day before, which is of course a huge benefit in many races.'

Things rarely, if ever, go one hundred per cent to plan at the Tour, however. The team may need to change its tactic following a race incident, like a crash, or after a response to a rival squad's unanticipated move, and that will affect what all the riders, or just some of them, consume.

'When the stage is much harder than we predicted,' Redegeld says, 'and they burn maybe one or two thousand calories more than what we planned then it's impossible to refuel that on the same day. Then we also do it a little bit on the next day. But especially during a Grand Tour, we really, really try to get them in energy balance every day, by the end of the day. Just to make sure they are recovered and fuelled optimally for the next stage.'

McEwen had no such thing as a food app during his career from 1996 to 2012 and shudders at the thought of it.

'You spend that much time on social media and apps and on your phone that something telling you when and what to eat seems normal these days,' he says. 'But that would have done my head in.

'When I feel like something, I want to be able to have it, and for me as a sprinter, not that I was a fatty or anything, but I guess I was also lucky I could be in condition and at my optimal race weight where I had the most power without really having to watch what I ate.'

Due to his physiology and metabolism, McEwen found he didn't have a problem being at his 'race weight'.

'It allowed me to allow all the things I enjoy, and that actually really helped,' he continues.

However, McEwen still had to monitor his condition, to be lithe enough to crest the same mountains as the title contenders of his era, arguably made harder given the prevalence of doping at the time, and to keep within the time limit to stay in the race and contest the flat stages, which did suit him.

'I found that I couldn't afford to get too light, or I lost power. So, I didn't concentrate on trying to have less calories or I don't eat ice-cream cake or chocolate or don't drink. I ate and drank everything I liked,' he says.

'And the amount of training I was doing, I was lean as

anything. There were veins on veins. Sometimes, for me, it was like I wasn't able to eat enough it felt like.'

Like riders on the Tour now, McEwen would eat seven meals a day, or three big ones and four small ones as he puts it. In not depriving himself of the things he wanted McEwen stayed happy, and a happy bike rider is a successful bike rider.

However, that wasn't the case for everyone.

'I've seen guys get underweight. I've seen guys with eating problems,' he says. 'I've seen what they're eating and not eating and trying to be as light as possible, watts per kilo and all that. You see them fade away in terms of physiology, and their results fade away, and it's not healthy.

'Their skin looks a bit grey, they look just terrible. Or guys who are, you see how lean and skinny they are, but you can see their frame is not meant to be that small. You can see it's a real battle it takes out of guys.

'It's trying to find that balance of what's the optimum weight and how can I drop weight, maintain watts.'

It is a battle not just in cycling but a lot of professional sports and the other side of that 'gain' is the increased susceptibility to become ill.

'Elite sport is not all that healthy,' McEwen says, 'because it's like trying to tune an F1 car; they go to the millimetre, to the tenth of a millimetre, finding aerodynamics, doing all the stuff. The athletes are pushing themselves to try and get the ultimate in performance.'

In cycling, weight is a sensitive subject. Sometimes riders who are said to have been underweight don't recognise that they are, or they do but it's not something they want to publicly broadcast or dwell on.

There are only a handful of riders who have disclosed to me what their weight, or 'ideal' race weight is.

I once interviewed Chris Froome in Tasmania where he'd joined then-teammate Porte for pre-season training.

It was grey and raining outside, so I met Froome at a cafe. He ordered a green tea for himself and shouted me a coffee. Froome was wearing a loose-fitting Sky team tracksuit and I mentioned that he looked fit. He quipped that he needed to lose weight.

When I say his tracksuit was loose-fitting, I mean it looked like the adult-size parka jacket my mum bought me when I was ten and said I would grow into.

Froome, who is 1.86 metres tall, went on to say his ideal race weight was around 67 kilograms, which was only a couple of kilos more than what I was packing at the time.

It was small talk before I formally started the interview, but I've never forgotten the conversation and, years later, speaking to Hayman, I return to it.

I ask Hayman if a cyclist must appear or be emaciated to compete at the Tour.

'Is it healthy?' Hayman repeats my question. 'Probably not. But this is the top of the top. It's the Tour de France and it's something I wanted. I wanted to be light.'

Hayman always did that extra bit for the Tour.

'If you were a kilo lighter it made that whole thing of chasing the *grupetto*, or being comfortably in it, or being one group in front of the *grupetto* – that's a kilo for each one of those scenarios – [easier].'

Hayman says he was not the only one, that it applied to all the 180-odd riders in the bunch. It's not totally different today, even with the scientific advances teams have made.

Redegeld believes Jumbo–Visma's app has a lot of important mental and physical performance benefits. 'The riders are really happy that they don't have to think about it themselves anymore,' he says.

'It was often a stress factor for many guys, and they were continuously in doubt if they had enough or not. And now they just know if they follow their app they have enough.'

It sounds like a bleak routine, eating what plain food you're told, when you're told. However, going off the results of a team that has become one of the big three in the WorldTour – boasting the likes of Primož Roglič, Wout van Aert and Tom Dumoulin in its ranks – the advantages are obvious.

Before lithe climber George Bennett left Jumbo–Visma at the end of the 2021 season to join Pogačar at UAE Team Emirates, he admitted the first thing he wanted to do after the 2020 Tour was turn the app off. That Tour Bennett was racing for Roglič, who lost the yellow jersey to Pogačar on the penultimate stage.

Bennett also never used the app during the off-season when he'd travel from Europe back to his native New Zealand for a break. 'I won't weigh a gram of food or worry about any of that until I come to Europe,' he says. 'Even at home [in Spain] I don't really do it, it's just when I'm with the team, when I'm doing team camps, the races, then I get on it.'

Equally, he sees the worth of the system.

'You see a lot of guys trying so hard to lose weight in stupid ways and they blow up or they just lose their power, whatever, they crack. But when you are training hard you need to be able to push the power and that's what is quite good about this app. It's never about losing weight, it's all about having enough power.'

The approach to nutrition at every team is different. There is no salary cap in cycling, so some teams have bigger budgets than others. Jumbo–Visma also uses Ketones, a controversial yet legal dietary supplement, which upwards of six teams were said to have consumed at the 2018 Tour.

Other squads are happy to not so intimately track how riders prepare, so long as they arrive at the Tour, or other races, ready.

Porte, who returned to Ineos Grenadiers in 2021 to see out the final two years of his career, happy to resume a super *domestique* role at the Tour, recognises that being underweight is still a danger in the sport.

'That's one thing I've really learned, even coming back to this team, is I've under-fuelled so much. You're worried about power-to-weight but at the end of the day you've still got to put the right fuel in at the right time,' he says.

McEwen intimates that the fine line both individuals and today's super teams tread, the difference between optimal and unhealthy, is physiology. He approaches the subject with a common-sense attitude everyone can relate to.

'That was one of the things I've said about Sky a lot, and now with Jumbo–Visma. The thing with the nutrition training and losing all this weight and using Ketones and everything, they strip right down to the bare minimum, they get in such good form, one hundred per cent of their capability. The problem is, how long can they hold it for?'

CHAPTER 4
THE ALPHA FROM AFRICA

The riders who compete to win the *maillot jaune* are the central protagonists of the Tour de France. For them especially there is no hiding. Every day they are in focus.

Their aim is to not lose time on stages that don't suit them – flat stages, time trials for some, medium mountain stages where there is a risk they can get caught out – and make up time or put time into rivals on stages that do suit them, usually in the high mountains where fans from all over the world, dizzy with excitement, having waited for hours in the elements to see a few minutes of action, are always eager for blood.

While a sprinter may work harder during the Tour, a yellow jersey contender can never lose concentration in the constant commotion that surrounds them.

They will sit at the front of a bunch during a flat stage until they are within three kilometres of the finish, where, according to UCI rules, they cannot lose time in the event of a crash or mechanical incident.

Even though the stories of title contenders are told daily, for me, they are the hardest riders to read and hold their cards closest to their chest.

Lance Armstrong's dictatorship at the Tour de France was before my time but I've interviewed him on camera once before. I can't remember a word he said, though he made a big impression. The seven-time *maillot jaune* winner turned disgraced drug cheat was sitting in a van at the 2010 Tour Down Under, and I asked him for an interview, three years before he admitted to doping in front of Oprah Winfrey.

He was teammates with Robbie McEwen then and had leaned over him to speak. Leaning over someone is generally considered rude but, given McEwen's stature, especially on home turf, it also felt awkward. I considered walking around to the window on the other side of the van, but I was young and instead chose to fire away while I still had the chance, without competing journalists around.

It was five years after his last Tour win in 2005, but Armstrong was still a persuasive boss. During that edition of Down Under he'd made a speech at a black-tie dinner, dressed in a tuxedo, the distinctive, yellow Livestrong arm bands of his charity a gift on every table. He was such a convincing public speaker that if he'd asked you to sign over your life savings to him you would have.

It was a contrast to the next year when the public's mood had begun to noticeably shift and he, on the precipice of being exposed, moved around in scruffy jeans and a T-shirt, surrounded often by an impenetrable entourage of burly men.

'Hey, Digger!' he said to me that day in 2010. It was in

friendly recognition of my nationality, not because I was digging for anything.

As Armstrong answered my questions, I watched him closely. He is still the only person I've ever interviewed who I would say can lie non-verbally. All athletes can lie. They may fib about a contract that hasn't been publicly announced yet, or their preparation, a tactic, personal circumstance, whatever. But, as the adage goes, ninety-nine per cent of communication is non-verbal and most people have tells.

With Armstrong on this day, however, every single one of his movements was orchestrated to emphasise a point he was making, or to match the general tone of the interview, which was happy even though the kindling that would later turn into a blaze and burn his metaphorical house down was already alight. Basically, he took control of the interview.

In the early years of my career, and even now, I would arrive early for sit-down or one-on-one interviews to scope out the room and change it around if necessary. When I was starting out, admittedly very naïve and innocent, this was important, particularly as a woman.

Sexism wasn't something I had really experienced until I began working as a journalist. I was aware of the rumours about me. That old 'she got that interview because she slept with him, or half the peloton' chestnut.

Now it's not an issue but at the time it would reduce me to tears, not least when I had to dissuade inappropriate advances, act like nothing had happened and still cop that. I felt like I had to work harder to prove myself and gain respect, especially when a former SBS colleague once put an exclusive I'd researched and worked hard for months on down to 'sex appeal'.

So, in one-on-one settings I would try to ensure that the room was suitable for having comfortable, open conversations on equal terms.

I'd do things like make sure the chairs were on level footing, so no one was sitting above or below the other, or not too far away but not too close.

The interview questions were always well-researched, brazen and designed to elicit answers that were not already known or had been circulated in the press. My aim is to walk away from an interview having learned or understood something real about the subject.

But with Armstrong, who older colleagues have described as a sociopath, I got absolutely nothing.

After the interview, I was annoyed because of this and went to find commentators Phil Liggett and the late Paul Sherwen. They had worked with Armstrong, or at least followed his career, for years and years, so I asked them.

'What's he actually like?'

Liggett said he didn't know.

At the time I remember perceiving that as a failure. How do you work with someone for so long and not know who they are?

However, I've since learned that the fight for the *maillot jaune* often involves smoke and mirrors, and mind games.

It was something that Cadel Evans said he had to learn during his racing career, to help deal with the pressure and expectation that surrounded his many title bids.

'To stay calm in a situation on the Tour, when you're there to win or lose, and you're playing games with your competitors, but also playing to win or lose the Tour de France with a guy like [Alberto] Contador, people like to gamble on things,' Evans explains.

'I don't gamble myself, but I have the ability to do that in certain occasions. Whether you're racing for a world title or a Tour de France, it's everything or nothing and you're playing with that to try and win the race. To stay calm in that situation, in a race situation, on the Galibier [mountain pass] or something, took quite a few years to learn.'

I'm reminded of the 2021 Tour when Ecuadorian rider Richard Carapaz looked like he was labouring behind Tadej Pogačar and Danish rider Jonas Vingegaard in the mountains on stage 18 from Pau to Luz Ardiden. The trio were leading the race, but Carapaz appeared to be in danger and refused to take a turn. He followed Pogačar and Vingegaard, who shared the pace-making, with gritted white teeth and a pained facial expression. Carapaz looked done, but I had an inkling something more was going on.

'So, is Carapaz not taking a turn because he's struggling or is he going to attack at the last minute and win the stage?' I posted on Twitter as the race unfolded.

And sure enough, with 1.4 kilometres remaining, Carapaz attacked. He lost steam and was overtaken, finishing third behind Pogačar and Vingegaard, but that day his expression had belied his condition. The performance no doubt contributed to his third place on general classification at the end of the Tour. After the Tour, he went on to win gold in the Tokyo Olympic Games men's road race.

If there is one team that has mastered the artistry of game-playing it is Carapaz's Ineos Grenadiers squad.

That may sound odd given that the team's playbook from

its first Tour victory in 2012 up until 2020 was no secret. In that time, it had one goal – to win the yellow jersey – with one man and everyone no matter their standing would commit to that endeavour. Once the team got the yellow jersey they then largely competed defensively, ever-present, lined out in single file at the front of the bunch, dictating terms to a point that, for a while, it seemed like rivals had resigned themselves to competing for minor places, not the win. They'd sit at the back of the train the British superpower would assemble and either couldn't, or wouldn't, attempt to attack; rather they'd just hold position.

But the team wasn't always forthcoming. When Bradley Wiggins won the yellow jersey in 2012, I discovered that asking for insight, with an Australian accent, was a tricky endeavour. The London Olympics quickly followed the Tour that year and teams had doubled down on the information they were willing to share, with me anyway.

I remember asking team principal David Brailsford, who was also in charge of British Cycling at the time, a question during the Tour about Wiggins's dual yellow jersey and Olympic gold bid.

'I'm not telling you anything with that accent,' Brailsford replied.

'Very funny,' I said, before realising he was serious.

It was the same with the Australians. I was Australian but working as British registered press. Access denied. American riders became my best friends that year.

I never got much out of Wiggins. My impression of him then was that he was more open when talking to older, hard men, not young women.

His yellow jersey victory kicked off a cycling craze in the UK. At one point, *The Sun* newspaper printed sideburn cut-outs replicating Wiggins's, which fans taped to their faces. In London, when people asked me what I did for a living, and I said cycling journalist, the questions about Wiggins flooded in, so much so I started saying I was a nurse.

Wiggins's performance, emphatic as it was, in 2012 wasn't what struck me most though.

Chris Froome was tasked with supporting Wiggins, who was five years his senior, at that edition and was clearly one of the strongest riders on the team and in the race, which he went on to finish second overall.

It was stage 17 and Froome and Wiggins were riding in a front group that had splintered on the slopes to Peyragudes, where they'd finish second and third, respectively, nineteen seconds behind Alejandro Valverde. My key recollection was not the result, or Wiggins realising he had more or less won yellow. Wiggins was the man for Sky that year. Sprinter Mark Cavendish was part of the squad and won three stages but reflecting on the Tour months later clearly felt muzzled, saying he, and Froome, could have won more and not to the detriment of Wiggins. But that wasn't the team's priority. On the last climb Wiggins and Froome were riding together, when the latter darted up the road, glancing back and gesturing at his teammate to follow.

There were many ways the move could have been, and was, interpreted but for me it was a clear statement of intent from Froome about his capability and desire.

Twelve months later, Froome arrived at the Tour as the leader of Team Sky, which recognised his step-up in performance.

It was the beginning of a new dynasty.

Speaking to him nine years later I come back to that moment on the mountain stage. Was I overreaching in thinking it was political by design? How did he usurp Wiggins, the national hero, who was so revered that he was knighted? Was there a frank conversation behind closed doors about the succession?

'Not really,' says Froome. 'It was an evolution.'

That evolution didn't begin at the 2012 Tour, rather at an event the year before: the 2011 Vuelta a España. Prior to that, Froome's best result at a Grand Tour was thirty-fifth at the 2009 Giro d'Italia with the Barloworld–Bianchi team. He'd competed at the Tour only once before his pointed 2012 showing with Sky, finishing eighty-first on race debut with Barloworld in 2008.

At the 2011 Vuelta everything came together for Froome, and at the right time, he recalls. It was the first time the Kenyan-born Briton had shown his Grand Tour aptitude, finishing second behind Juan José Cobo, with Wiggins rounding out the podium. Froome was later awarded the title after Cobo was retrospectively stripped of his results over an anti-doping violation.

'It was pretty apparent during the 2011 Vuelta that I had the ability to ride GC,' Froome says. 'And immediately at the end of that Vuelta, when it came to renewing the contract with the [Sky] team, I basically said this is something I want to do: I want to ride GC at the Tour de France, I believe I've got what it takes, and that's the direction I want to go with my career.'

Froome attributes his improvement to three factors – home life, weight and health. In 2011, he settled in Monaco after years of moving around, so had a stable base from which to work. Losing weight was also a huge catalyst. Froome typically raced at around 70 to 71 kilograms but for that Vuelta he had dropped down to under 68 kilograms, which benefited him in the high mountains where he had in the past struggled.

'I'd always seen that I had an engine in time trials, but I could never really go the distance on the long climbs,' he says.

Then there was his health. Months before the 2011 Vuelta, Froome had discovered he was suffering from bilharzia – a disease caused by parasitic worms – which had affected his form.

'I'd build up to a point and just get sick immediately, so finding out that I had that and getting rid of that parasite was a big part of it.'

Froome went on to win the *maillot jaune* in 2013, 2015, 2016, 2017, and was third in 2018, when teammate Geraint Thomas triumphed. He is one title victory short of equalling cycling legends Eddy Merckx, Jacques Anquetil, Bernard Hinault and Miguel Indurain, who have won the most Tours at five each. Armstrong may still hold on to his seven yellow jerseys, but the American's victories were stripped from record.

There was no apparent hostility between Thomas and Froome in 2018, as there ultimately was with Wiggins. At a function in London at the end of the 2018 season Froome and Thomas were asked to interview each other in front of an intimate crowd. Froome asked Thomas a polite question, which I can't recall. Thomas asked Froome tongue-in-cheek what he thought of Wiggins, who was invited but didn't show. Thomas did so much media throughout the earlier stages of the 2018 Tour that I was convinced Froome, despite not appearing as strong, was still the designated leader until his teammate, suited to the shorter mountain stages that defined the edition rode into yellow.

Thomas is a laid-back Welshman with a dry sense of humour. Prior to his Tour triumph he had already made a name for himself as an Olympic track gold medallist, classics man and handy stage racer, having come through the British Cycling academy.

Froome is nothing like Armstrong was with me that day at the Tour Down Under, or in general. He is not a sociopath and in one-on-one interviews over the years has provided tidbits into his character.

In a TV interview once I asked him, considering he was raised in Kenya, if he spoke Swahili.

He did.

I asked if he could say something to camera in Swahili.

He hesitated, but then obliged with a quick verse.

Froome races under a British licence and represents Team GB at international meets like the Olympics and World Championships. However, his accent is true to his upbringing.

He's multilingual, and rivals also recall his ability to speak in Spanish and French, so you'd imagine he's a good communicator in the bunch. English is the common language in the peloton now but speaking in native tongues, especially when fatigue sets in, is less exhausting, more welcome and clearer.

Froome has always given me his time and I respect him. But I still perceive him to be a bit of an enigma because, as a journalist, I've never been able to fully crack through his exceptional manners, which are genuine, but also a veneer.

'He says all the right things and he's boring,' Richie Porte says of his former teammate's approach to the press. 'Whereas, when you get him off the bike, he talks about catching snakes, or being chased by hippos and stuff like that as a kid. He's awesome.'

I'd always figured there was more underneath his polite and eloquent surface so I'll never forget that time we sat down for green tea and coffee in Tasmania and with a cheeky smile and twinkle in his eye, Froome described his then teammate and confidante Porte as a 'little cunt'.

It is the only time I've heard Froome break from the sort of straight, courteous demeanour that would make any parent proud, but which infuriates me.

The formative stories I've heard about Froome aren't like those of his British counterparts. There are no photos of him as a boy getting his picture taken with a pro at a bike race; he didn't grow up with Thomas and other former Sky and Ineos Grenadiers teammates, many of whom were reared through and graduated from British Cycling.

Froome, legend has it, used to go spearfishing at the same age, and initially took up cycling not because he knew or cared for the long history of the Tour, or figures like Merckx and Hinault, who Wiggins so revered. No, his affinity with bikes was far more liberating.

'From a young age I always just loved being on a bike, but it was never about racing,' he says. 'It was a mode of transport for me and a way to experience the world as a kid growing up in Africa.

'It was my wings, really, my way to get out and experience the world.'

When it became more than that, Froome, coming from

Kenya, attended the UCI World Cycling Centre – a training and racing facility in Switzerland that the sport's governing body oversees.

'Only as a late teenager did it become about training to become better, to be better in racing. But I think, certainly, forming that bond and love for cycling early on in my life – that's played a huge part in it,' he says.

To get to where Froome is now – four Tour de France victories, one Giro d'Italia and two Vuelta a España titles – you don't have to echo Armstrong's attitude, but it does take more than saying please and thank you.

One thing that is strikingly obvious about Froome is his mental resilience in victory and defeat.

After his career-threatening crash at the 2019 Critérium du Dauphiné, Froome was in the pool about a month later already rehabilitating. He was back on the road competing in February the next year at the UAE Tour. He wasn't at the top of his game but his return so soon after a major crash was a testament to his tenacity. So too was the fact that pundits expected more.

At the UAE Tour an editor messaged me asking if I could write a story about why Froome, eight months after his crash, was 'so shit'. When I read the message, I stopped in my tracks and then conferred with a colleague. Had I gone soft or was that comment a tad unfair?

Froome at the Dauphiné had crashed on a recon ride of the time trial route and suffered from multiple injuries including a fractured neck, fractured right femur, a broken hip and fractured ribs.

I would not write that he was underperforming.

In victory, as a yellow jersey winner and contender, you are loved as much as you are simultaneously hated at the Tour. Fans will deafen riders with cheers of adoration one day and get dirty from the roadside the next. In 2015 Froome claimed a spectator threw a small cup of urine at him and yelled 'doper' during stage 14.

The media will build you into a Goliath and then query if your performances are legitimate and trustworthy, because of the sport's past.

Froome has weathered those storms with skin as thick as the bony plates of an armoured armadillo. The words that have rendered some of his rivals unstuck don't hurt him.

'I'm aware of it but it really doesn't feature much on my radar at all. I don't get fazed by much,' Froome says of public criticism. 'I've got such a single-minded focus when I'm in that race for GC. I've got such a single-minded focus on the job at hand that I don't really pay much attention to the noise around me.'

Froome has spoken up about public mistreatment after an event, but in the race I can't imagine him ever approaching me, as others have, to remonstrate over something I've broadcast or written.

'Mentally you have to be extremely strong,' he says. 'It goes without saying physically you have to have the goods – that comes down to preparation, all the training and everything building up to that point – but that's just to be in the arena, to be a contender.

'Once you have that,' Froome continues, 'to actually win the race comes down to mental resilience and how you can deal with unforeseen circumstances, how you can deal with setbacks.

'On top of that, you need a bit of luck as well for things not to go completely tits up.'

Froome keeps close counsel. When we speak in the lead-up to the 2021 Tour a lot has changed, and not just because of the pandemic.

Froome had left Ineos Grenadiers after a ten-year tenure to join Israel Start-Up Nation, with which he was returning to the Tour following a two-year absence due to injuries stemming from the Dauphiné crash.

An Israel Start-Up Nation team press officer had handed my interview request over to Froome's wife, Michelle, who vetted which organisations I was working for, the questions I wanted to ask and coordinated a time to speak. They're a team. There is no big-noting sports agent, no commercial manager, no specially assigned team staffer to go through. But it is a formal and controlled process.

After all these years, I want to ask Froome what is behind his insatiable drive and motivation. Winning one Tour is, to a degree, explanatory, winning four and defining an era is something else. To my knowledge Froome, who has the biggest following on social media of any active male road cyclist, posting to an audience of 1.5m on Twitter and 1.1m on Instagram, has never spoken of wanting to leave a legacy, of caring if he's in the history books alongside glorified cycling greats, of a desire for fame.

I'm in Paris days before the 2021 Grand Depart when Michelle calls and then passes the phone to her husband. Froome is at home in Monaco, preparing to leave for the Tour.

This time, just getting to Paris after a long injury comeback, which an almost five-month industry-wide competition shutdown at the onset of the COVID-19 pandemic encumbered, is the objective, not the yellow jersey.

I have fifteen minutes.

'I wouldn't necessarily say the glory,' Froome says of what motivates him.

'But having said that, I do have a very competitive side in that I love being able to train for a goal, to go through all the sacrifices, the dedication to training, and see the results of that training paying off in racing.

'I love that mindset, if you like, the whole regime of going away, getting your body physically to a point and then to come into a race environment and show what you've got.

'I genuinely do enjoy that,' Froome continues, 'and if I didn't, I wouldn't be able to still carry on, and at this point of my career.'

He continues, 'When I'm in that race mode, it doesn't matter what it is, basically the result takes precedence over everything.'

His focus at the Tour is resolute, his execution precise. Cycling is his livelihood and when he steps on the bike his rivals are no longer people; rather, like those fish he apparently used to spear in his spare time, they are prey.

CHAPTER 5
CAPTAINS OF THE ROAD

Winners comprise the narrative of the Tour de France each year but only one or two – and at best three – athletes from each of the teams that compete are written into legend, their bloody battles celebrated and documented in lights for the masses.

The rest are like movie extras. In the background, they suffer in silence, their stories on the same unforgiving roads rarely told, their pain and sacrifice not rewarded with shots at personal glory, adoration, or riches, which help to absolve the agony.

The first thing teams do when they roll in to a stage start is hold a meeting. Before the pandemic, I would stand, among many others, waiting and waiting by team buses for the conferences to end and faces to emerge.

The insides of the buses serve as sanctuaries for riders. Sponsor logos and advertisements are plastered on the sides and back of the customised coaches so that the riders can see out but you can't see in, and a blind is usually pulled down low across the front windscreen to maximise their privacy.

Riders who are leading a classification, like the green or yellow jersey, are also presented with stuffed toys on the podium each day, and teams line the toys along the bus's dashboard as an advertisement of how things are going.

I've only been inside a team bus once or twice at the Tour and both times it was in the third week, when even the leather seats smelled like a men's locker room, no matter how tidy and clean everything else was.

For Mathew Hayman the bus was a special place, showcasing the best and worst of the people he worked with during the Tour.

'We've got eight guys, it used to be nine, in a bus with a director, a swanny [*soigneur*] and a bus driver,' he says. 'It's a pretty confined space and we end up spending a lot of hours on there. We do need to keep it tidy and be respectful of each other's space, but there's not a lot of it going around.'

As the race grinds on, the bus, by Hayman's account, starts to sound like more of a share house. With eight riders all faring differently, no one goes to or comes home from work every day happy.

Hayman preferred to be left alone the first twenty minutes after a stage had finished.

'I'm a pretty bad sore loser and I hate losing, and we don't win very often at Tour de France,' Hayman laughs. 'So, I'm not normally in a good mood.

'By the end of three weeks people are spending a bit more time with earplugs in and switching off.'

Hayman competed at the Tour always under the tutelage of Matt White.

'Whitey, let's say ninety-nine per cent of the time, he's great for the environment on the bus,' he says. 'He's playing music, having a laugh and, even when things are going well, or bad, he knows we have to keep that fun environment. And it also wears thin on a few people at some point but if we are all sitting there with glum faces and misery, sometimes you have to, whatever is lying ahead.'

Inside the bus, riders must make concessions, and not just when it comes to musical taste, like the pop rock that used to blare from former world champion and seven-time green jersey winner Peter Sagan's Bora–hansgrohe bus. Teams spend countless hours driving in them from stage to stage, and hotel to hotel – competing, eating and sleeping in between.

'What might be a miserable day for me might be someone else's favourite day in the Tour de France,' Hayman continues. 'They might be heading into a mountain stage, and I'm dreading it and couldn't think of anything worse, and one of the climbers has picked this day out three weeks ago and was looking forward to it.

'You have to respect each other a little bit there but, definitely by the end of it, I've thrown a few things in the bus and kicked someone's shoes out the door – and they know who they are – if they won't clean up and leave shit all over the place.'

After the pre-stage meetings have finished, everyone starts to get ready for the day ahead and eventually emerge from inside the bus. There is a roll call effectively at the start of every stage called sign on, and the riders must scrawl their signature next to their name or race number to confirm they're present. Some like to do this straight away and then ride back to the bus to wait for the start of the race there. Others leave it until the last minute and then stay at the start line ready to roll out. Amongst that the riders will speak to press and sign autographs for fans also.

The buses are kept running at the stage starts, I assume so the air-con stays on inside, the toilet flush works and the laundry machines concealed under the carriage can be used.

Standing outside them waiting for a rider that you needed to interview to come out was usually an exercise in patience. The diesel fumes emanating from the exhaust would make the air feel hotter and before the pandemic when media could roam freely you always had to be mindful of your physical position, so as not to lose your spot and miss talking to someone.

Despite the daily team meetings, even the best laid plans at the Tour don't always work out and the dynamics inside the peloton are different to those inside the bus.

The sports directors can lay out a strategy in the morning, they can provide guidance, information, and motivation from the car in the convoy, which travels behind the peloton, or breakaway, but the riders themselves do the work.

The road captains of the Tour are especially aware of this.

There are two different types of team leaders at the Tour. There are the winners – the blinkered sprinters, *puncheurs* and climbers, one-minded title contenders fixated on their own, individual ambitions. And there are the road captains – often intelligent, strong communicators, generally grounded, likeable, and influential.

Every team has a road captain, they may not be the most well-known cyclist, but they are usually strong, experienced riders. They hold sway within their own team and other times their authority extends to the peloton at large. Mark Cavendish when he competed with skippers Michael Rogers and Bernhard Eisel used to say it was Mick and Bernie's peloton.

The scope of captains extends from making calls on the road about how to ride, positioning and communicating that to their teammates, to dropping back from the peloton to the sports directors in the team car to get extra *bidons* (drink bottles) for everyone, which they stuff underneath the back and sides of their jersey until there is no more space and then ride back to the bunch and distribute.

'It's all well and good going over [strategy] on a team bus and being given instructions but executing them and remembering every detail in the middle of a washing machine, whirlwind, bike race is another thing again,' says experienced road captain Simon Clarke.

'There's a certain amount that the directors can do from the car but there's also a certain amount that you need to just be able to read on the road and study.

'You need to go through each stage on Google Earth and highlight any dangerous areas and remember them, and make sure you guide your leader through those areas safely, so he's ready to contest the decisive climbs, which is where most of the time the race is decided.'

Clarke's campaign at the 2021 Tour was indicative of how quickly momentum can shift. When we speak on the second rest day, the clean-cut Australian sounds so weary that I wonder if his press officer has a gun to his head, forcing him to do the interview on the other end of the line.

'I crashed three times every day for the first three days, so I didn't have a good run and I've been pretty much trying to hide and carry the consequences of those three crashes through the Tour,' Clarke says.

'As a result, it's been a Tour of survival for me [rather] than chasing any dreams or objectives.'

Clarke is used to being part of the backbone of a team as a road captain at the Tour, not competing with a broken back, which scans later showed he had. Nevertheless, he made it to Paris amid reports questioning the financial stability of his then Qhubeka NextHash team, which months later proved true, and the squad folded.

In previous years at the Tour, Clarke had worked for Colombian title contender Rigoberto Uran at team EF Education–First.

'That kind of really raised the stakes for me in terms of taking leadership in the group and making sure everything went smoothly, seeing as though such a good result was at stake,' he says.

Uran doesn't speak English, so Clarke was also a conduit for me to understand the Colombian.

As a captain he is relied upon for tasks that often go unnoticed but are crucial in the day to day of the Tour. Clarke didn't have the same position, protecting a title contender, at the 2021 edition, which Qhubeka NextHash entered with an opportunistic approach, but, despite being injured, he still felt drawn to continue the race out of responsibility.

'[Teams have] relied a lot on me to lead the guys on the road and take a bit of leadership and I can still do that in the racing,' Clarke says. 'And so, I feel like there's still value for me to be here even if I am the walking wounded.'

Previously with Uran he may have been focused on the

mountain stages but in 2021 it was about getting into more competitive breakaways, which towards the end of the Tour Clarke himself did.

'I've helped facilitating, making sure that the right guys get in the breakaways and the right guys are in the breakaways, and just being as competitive as possible with the team,' Clarke continued.

The road captains of the Tour are the eyes of the team. Clarke is well-researched, calm and always prepared. In his years competing for Uran he was sometimes the only team member who would do a cool down after a stage outside EF's bus. I never rushed to speak to him because I knew he'd be there, on the rollers, religiously following his routine.

Being a team captain is an unassuming job that Australian Luke Durbridge has come to pride himself on at BikeExchange–Jayco.

The squad has changed its orientation at the Tour several times. It started as an opportunistic team comprised of mainly sprinters and classics specialists focused on stage wins, then made moves to become a concerted general classification squad, recruiting climbers who could contest for the yellow jersey. In recent years it has turned its focus again, recruiting Michael Matthews and Dutch sprint superstar Dylan Groenewegen. Durbridge for every one of those has had to at the look at the big picture and get his team leaders – be they sprinters, title contenders or *puncheurs* – in the safest, best position possible, which changes with the direction of outfit.

The tall and broad Western Australian grew up playing team sports and considers himself a big team player. He's too classy a character to be cast in the A-Team but loves it when a plan comes together.

Durbridge has the same studied approach as Clarke and enjoys the planning process, seeing every stage of the Tour from all vantage points and navigating it.

'So, the intricacies of starting two hundred and fifty kilometres from victory, and how you're going to get there,' Durbridge says.

'And I really like, from kilometre zero to two hundred and fifty kilometres, every little intricacy along the way – studying the course, knowing which corner is going to have wind, which is not, what you need nutrition [wise]. All of these little details I really enjoy, and I really enjoy pushing my body to the limit.

'That's why I find it rewarding because it is a team sport, but it is also very individual in aspects as well. I like the mix of it. It's a really beautiful sport.'

Aside from a studious knowledge of stage routes and race conditions, Durbridge also takes a personable approach to the task.

'You've just got to think what's best for your leader, get to know them personally and how they work in the bunch. Do they like to ride back in the peloton, or do they like to ride safely at the front? What do they do? What do they like to eat, drink, all this sort of stuff,' he says.

'It's something I've worked over the years to get good at and something I really enjoy. It gives me great pride to help teammates out, especially some of the leaders I've worked with in the past – they're just really fantastic people and I'm very grateful.'

Durbridge may sound like an optimist, a dreamer, but he's

been in the sport for a long time and he's also a realist. When I ask if liking or at least respecting the leader of the team, the person he not only rides for but also anticipates the needs and safety of, is essential, he laughs.

'Not necessarily,' Durbridge says.

'In the end that's what your job is. If you simplify it, that's what you get paid to do and that's what they get paid to do.'

He continues, 'Sometimes it can be like that, but I'd say ninety per cent of the time, probably more ninety-five per cent of the time, they're just great guys.'

Durbridge is a team player at the Tour but outside of it, at other races during the season, he gets opportunities to vie for personal results. He's a former national time trial champion and has a good go at the spring classics.

'I know what rider I am, and what I can do, and I don't win as much as most or some, so I need to focus on what I'm good at for this period of time and then when I get an opportunity take it,' he says at the Tour.

Durbridge is selfless in his summation of the job. He doesn't speak of his own abilities within the Tour team, or what he brings to the table, just how much he enjoys what he does.

The best teams at the Tour communicate well and you don't have to be behind the scenes to witness that. Watch any stage on TV and you're likely to see an Ineos Grenadiers rider drawing their chin down across their chest to talk into a radio piece hidden under their jersey.

Road captains can direct a large part of that chat, but rarely do you hear of them outside those thirty-second interview clips that the winner gives at the end of every stage, in which they thank their collective teammates.

When the Tour is over, the winner may buy their teammates gifts, watches or tokens in appreciation, but you don't put yourself through a month of physical hell and mental torment for a timepiece.

When I ask George Bennett, a Grand Tour contender in his own right, how he became inspired to work for Slovenian contender and three-time Vuelta a España winner Primož Roglič at the 2020 Tour, it wasn't, he says, in any way related to personal acknowledgement.

'If you did the sport for acknowledgement, you probably wouldn't feel very fulfilled,' Bennett says.

'I think it's more you become quite invested in the goal, you know what I mean. I don't know why, I guess you just spend enough time training with people.'

Bennett raced with incarnations of Jumbo–Visma for seven years before he transferred to join UAE Emirates ahead of the 2022 season. His long tenure at the squad spoke to his general motivation.

'I've been in teams where I wasn't invested in the goal because I didn't believe in it, I didn't particularly like the person,' Bennett says. 'That's quite important to me, all that stuff, actually. And having a leader that's a good guy and things like that makes a big difference and makes you realise, when I'm leading, how important that stuff is – to be personable with your teammates, build a strong off-the-bike relationship – because you can get so much more out of them. The same way people get more out of me if I like them.'

There are many big personalities in cycling and anyone who tells you they don't have enemies is either new or a liar. It's not possible in an environment like the Tour to be amicable every day. And sometimes we all must work with people we don't like. Even though Bennett is a straight shooter, he gets that.

'If I don't get on with them of course I'll do my job. At the end of the day, it is a job; you're getting paid,' he says.

'But will you ride through a foot that you can't walk on and broken ribs and a shoulder you can't hold the handlebars properly [with]?

'Do you ride through that for a guy that you don't like, or you don't really care if they win or lose? Maybe not. But if there's an investment there on a personal level you can always get more out of yourself.' They were the injuries Bennett carried at the 2020 Tour after a bad crash on stage 1.

At Jumbo–Visma that level of investment became a vibe.

Bennett was on the road with the Tour team for months in the lead-up to the race and the momentum they generated en route carried through.

'I think it was just the whole team environment that we'd been together, we were flying, we were a good group of guys, we'd been to the races before and just been dominating,' Bennett recalls. 'It was this cool wave we were riding.'

He continues, 'Once you become the best team it's harder to stay there, for sure, but there is, in much the way that there was that group in Sky in the late Wiggins, early Froome days, those guys were just killing everything.

'When you're winning everyone is happy, it's exciting, you want to be part of this group and you become invested in it, you see how hard everyone is working, the sacrifices everyone is making, and you get on board with the vibe.

'If you don't, you won't be in the Tour team or around for long, at least I'd say.'

The collective gain at the team also became collective pain. The photos of Roglič's teammates watching Tadej Pogačar blast through the time trial on the penultimate stage to steal the yellow jersey are testament to that. Tom Dumoulin's face, for example, appeared just as devastated as that of three-time stage winner Roglič, who had been a day away from winning his first *maillot jaune*.

Bennett loves the Tour. As a rising Grand Tour title contender, it's a race he's not shying away from one day having a crack at himself.

'It's why I ride a bike, it's my dream, it's what I want to do and eventually try and have the best result I can at the Tour; I'm all about the Tour,' he says.

So, it's another level of investment again when you consider that he, and magnanimous champions like Dumoulin, who has won the Giro d'Italia and is routinely sought at the Tour, went all-in for Roglič.

It's something Jumbo–Visma, Bennett says, communicated very clearly and well before the race started that year.

'I think everybody acknowledged, okay, we're a team stacked with guys that would potentially be leaders on any other team – at least four or five of us,' Bennett recalls. 'We didn't just go to the Tour and go, "Okay, here's a leader." We did a lot of talks, a lot of sit-downs before the Tour.

'I mean, they sat me down well before the Tour and said, "Look, we really want you on the Tour squad, but we only want you on the Tour squad if you are happy to give away [your chances]. You're not going to have a chance here, you're not going to go in a breakaway, you're not going for a stage, you're not going to do anything. You're going to go there and be a helper. If you're sweet with that, we'd love to have you in the Tour team, but please tell us if you're not and we'll put you in the Giro still, or whatever, but we really need to know that everyone is on the same page here."

'And they gave that talk to everybody … and assembled a Tour team from there.'

Bennett crashed twice during the opening stage of the 2020 Tour that was lashed with rain, which made the roads around Nice like a Slip N Slide. He was seen clutching his shoulder after falling on a descent with about 30 kilometres of the 156-kilometre stage remaining, and then was helped back to his bike when he came down again inside the last three kilometres.

The environment at Jumbo-Visma served as impetus to push on despite his injuries.

'It was a really strange race for me because I had the form of my life coming into it and then I crashed super hard, one of the hardest crashes I've had, on day one, and broke my ribs and injured my shoulder and my foot. And so, I had this weird thing where I was like personally suffering like hell for three weeks,' Bennett says.

'But on the other hand, it was such good guys, we had such a good atmosphere in the team, and we had such a goal that we were all so committed to, it eased the suffering a bit, made it all worth it.'

The influence road captains have is understated but powerful. Cadel Evans was boosted by the presence of George Hincapie during his title victory campaign.

They are a bit like an older brother or sister who can see further ahead. Calm, wise and willing to step in for you, to make the big calls en route and have your back.

CHAPTER 6
MR GREEN

Peter Sagan became so accustomed to wearing, and so synonymous with, the green jersey at the Tour de France that it looked weird when he didn't have it on.

For the better part of a decade, if you wanted to spot Sagan in the peloton, you'd just look for the green jersey, or the *maillot vert* as it is otherwise known.

The Slovakian ushered in a new era when he won the points classification for the first time in 2012. Up until then, as I'd known it, the points classification was usually contested by pure sprinters. Mark Cavendish had won it the season before, Alessandro Petacchi in 2010 and Thor Hushovd in 2009.

Outside of stage wins, the green jersey is the highest honour for sprinters, who Robbie McEwen is adamant work harder than anyone else at the Tour.

'As a sprinter, you suffer a lot more in the Tour to finish it compared to a climber because you're not suited to the course like they are,' says McEwen.

'The climbers they can ride a flat stage and just cruise in the bunch, and riding in with the bunch is really easy compared to being at the front trying to race for the stage win in a sprint.

'And then when you get to the hilly days, a medium day, they're doing it pretty easy. In the high mountains generally they're doing it pretty easy, for at least half the stage, and then they start to go in the red and really start to race.

McEwen continues, 'Where the sprinters are racing from the very first moment the road goes up because you're trying to get into the *grupetto* and you ride actually in sub-red zone all day long, and sometimes well over and into the red zone when you're trying to get back into the *grupetto*.

'The *grupetto* always sounds like it's the easy place to be. Well it ain't. Not when you're a non-climber.'

But Sagan's stranglehold on green became such that the fast men of the peloton began to dismiss it as an objective, until Sam Bennett's triumph in 2021, which sparked a revival of interest.

Between 2012 and 2021, Sagan won the *maillot vert* a record seven times. No one could wrestle it from his shoulders from 2012 to 2016.

In 2017, when Sagan was aiming for a record sixth consecutive victory, he was disqualified from the Tour following a high-speed crash involving Cavendish about 200 metres from the finish line of stage 4.

I was standing on the roadside at finish line when the crash unfolded.

I was freelancing for SBS that year and couldn't phone the producer, who would have been looking after the live broadcast, so had to make a call in that moment. Continue my original assignment – B-Roll of Richie Porte, which the cameraman and I had a lot of already and could easily get another time – or speak to every sprinter and lead-out specialist available about what had just happened between two of the biggest names in the sport. I found my cameraman and gave him the new instruction.

Sweat was dripping from Adam Hansen's brow when he pulled over to speak to us just metres past the finish line. Hansen has an engine. He holds the record for competing in the highest consecutive number of Grand Tours and was a deputy for German sprinter André Greipel, who won 11 stages at the Tour and on this day placed third behind French winner Arnaud Démare and runner-up Alexander Kristoff.

Under the glare of the sun, Hansen recovered his breath as he spoke into the TV microphone I was holding out after what would become one of the most hotly debated race incidents of that season.

The testosterone around us was palpable as Hansen spoke softly, answering all my questions in measured terms without a hint of insult across his face. What he saw, and I didn't know, was that mid-interview my cameraman, who was meant to be glued behind me, had left without a word when he saw Porte. If I wasn't red from the heat and adrenaline, I was from embarrassment when I turned around at the end of the interview to see no one filming behind me.

I went to Porte's bus where the cameraman was basically alone and asked what the fuck he was doing. It was chaos outside of Sagan's and Cavendish's camps. They were, even more so than the stage winner Démare, unless you were French, the story.

Tempers were flaring everywhere.

I tried to maintain my cool despite what happened with

Hansen and said we needed to run, literally run, to Cavendish's bus, which a surging swarm of people had gathered outside of.

He struggled to keep up and I'd stop and usher him to hurry. We'd miss out on a spot close enough to get a question in, or even the shot if he didn't.

A flimsy black, retractable band separated the Dimension Data team bus Cavendish was within from the reporters outside.

I'd pushed through the lines-deep crowd as far as I could and if I hyperextended my arm, the mic was close enough to pick up audio. There was now noise about Sagan getting not just penalised but disqualified and ejected from the race, and Cavendish potentially having to abandon the Tour due to injury, which he ultimately did with a fractured shoulder blade.

We waited as Dimension Data sports director Roger Hammond emerged first, his fuming a bit over the top. The Englishman huffed and puffed; his fists clinched as he apparently went to speak to the *commissaires* about the incident. *Commissaires* are the umpires, or referees, in cycling. They get paid a small daily allowance but are essentially volunteers.

Soon after Cavendish walked off the bus, with his hand wrapped in a white bandage that was stained with bright red blood.

There was an immediate response in the media pack as he came out and everyone was pushed forward. I couldn't tell if my feet were on the ground, or on someone else's leg and had to move with it, hoping that I wouldn't fall forward and get trampled. The arms of reporters standing behind me were outstretched across and rested on my shoulders, and even my head.

Cavendish was forced to take a step back and called for calm before answering a handful of questions. I got the last one in.

Did he think Sagan should be punished for closing him into the barriers?

He said he'd leave it to the judges, who his sports directors were still conferring with well after the stage had finished.

Sagan had finished second in the sprint and was initially relegated and docked eighty points from his green jersey total, but upon further video analysis, and probably a lot of posturising with judges, the penalty was upped.

He contested the disqualification, and the next morning I and a more manageable number of journalists had arrived at his hotel to learn the verdict.

Sagan was world champion that year and an identity of the Tour. There was also a lot of conjecture as to whether he really was at fault. He was disqualified for causing the crash, holding his elbow out in the sprint, basically, but I was among those who believed it was a race incident. In my view it was a bit of a cross-generational ego battle. Cavendish had tried to find a gap between Sagan and the barriers and Sagan held his ground, and his posture, sprinting with his arms locked out beside him. Maybe Cavendish was used to people bowing and giving way to him but so was Sagan and at that stage of his career especially was never going to move.

A *soigneur* emerged from the hotel and walked towards where the team cars were parked with a suitcase and a white mesh laundry bag that Sagan's rainbow jersey, still with race numbers attached, had been stuffed into. The verdict was clear.

Sagan eventually came out to meet us on the hotel gardens dressed in casual team kit; his shoulder-length hair untamed and made a statement. His disqualification would not be overturned, and he was going home to Monaco.

'I can accept the decision but for sure I do not agree with them, because I think I have done nothing wrong,' he said. 'As you saw it was a crazy sprint, it was not the first one like that or the last one.'

Speaking four years after the event, Sagan's former Bora–hansgrohe sports director, Enrico Poitschke, still didn't agree with the decision that spoiled his rider's unbeaten run of green jersey victories.

'He won already the jersey eight times in my eyes,' Poitschke says.

Sagan pursued legal action against the UCI, which was dropped in December when the federation reasoned the crash was an unintentional race incident.

Unbeknown to anyone, Michael Matthews, in his first season with Sunweb, had spent almost a year working on a project to win the green jersey in the 2017 Tour, and would go on to do so after a fierce contest with Marcel Kittel.

'It was one hundred per cent the focus,' says Matthews. 'We kept it out of the media a little bit, we didn't want to put a lot of media attention towards it, but we knew everything we had to do. We knew exactly which stages suited me, where I'd probably gain points, where I'd lose points, all the intermediates, we knew everything.'

Sagan went on to claim the *maillot vert* again in 2018 and 2019, becoming one of the biggest commercial entities in the sport. His scalps outside of the Tour include, but are not limited to, three world championships, Paris-Roubaix, the Tour of Flanders, and stage wins at the Giro d'Italia and Vuelta a España.

He has one of the biggest supporter bases at the Tour and took an entourage with him, including his older brother Juraj Sagan, when he left Bora–hansgrohe for team Total Direct Energie ahead of the 2022 season.

Matthews and Sagan have similar attributes compared to pure sprinters.

Pure sprinters are accustomed to and fixated on winning lots. For some, if they don't feel like they're at the head of a bunch kick, able to take line honours, they'll just sit up as opposed to push on for a minor place.

Sagan's attitude when it came to the green jersey was different. He always appeared focused on the long game. He wins less than pure sprinters but is a more versatile rider and handles undulating terrain. He knows he's not the fastest in a bunch sprint, but you'll be hard pressed to find a photo of a mass gallop without his face in frame. He could be second, third, fourth, fifth, it doesn't matter, he's not down or deterred. As long as it contributes towards the green jersey, it is a win.

He also went during his reign where pure sprinters could not. Sagan would ride almost outside of himself to reach an intermediate prime located on a part of the route that his quicker rivals would deem too hard and not bother with. He won the green jersey in 2014 without claiming a stage.

I was on the back of a motorbike one year at the Tour when I came upon Sagan riding solo in no-man's-land, between the breakaway and the peloton, neither of which was in sight. It was so unbearably hot that the sun was bouncing off exposed sandy rock around us and the skinny black jeans I was wearing were burning my skin. The heat was so bad that I was contemplating asking my driver to pull over so I could get off, wait on the roadside for the convoy and jump in an air-conditioned car, but then I was distracted.

'Go, Peter! Go, Peter!' my driver shouted with exuberance when he spotted Sagan.

We idled alongside Sagan as he laboured up a hill. He turned his head left towards us and, seeing his face, I forgot about everything else.

He looked like he was under a spell, grunting, his olive skin saturated in sweat. But it was his eyes that I still can't accurately describe. It was like they were possessed. That's the only way I can think to explain it. Sagan was clearly in discomfort. His eyes were glazed over and vacant, but he was also, evidently, fixated on something, the intermediate prime, wherever it was.

'The last years that always happens, especially in the flat and very easy stages, we have some guys faster,' says Poitschke. 'But with his energy and special talent, what he has had for the last years, he was stronger the whole Tour than other riders. That's why he was able to catch so many times the green jersey.'

In his winning 2017 campaign, Matthews also placed an emphasis on the intermediate primes.

'Probably me and Sagan have a very similar strategy to the green jersey,' says Matthews. 'Where Sam and Cavendish are more pure sprinters where they have to try and win as many flat stages as they can and then try and make sure the breakaways don't go away without them in it because that's where me and Sagan were getting a lot of our points.'

Even when Sagan was disqualified Matthews faced a serious challenge in Kittel, who could make up a lot of ground winning flat stages. Kittel was the pure sprinter of reference in the peloton at that point. His styled, blond locks were almost as renowned as he was. In 2017 he won five stages in the first twelve days.

'It was going to be quite an aggressive green jersey to fight for, I knew I wasn't the fastest sprinter with Kittel just dominating everyone that year in the pure flat sprints,' Matthews says.

'I knew I had to make him work really hard, to try and either get rid of him out of the race or try and score so many points in stages that he wasn't there that we could really make up the points we were losing on the pure flat stages.'

Matthews came to love the more multifaceted competition of racing for the green jersey over stage wins alone.

'When I was chasing all the points for the intermediates, I enjoyed it much more because every day you had something to do,' Matthews says.

'You never really had a day off, which I enjoy much more because you're always on your toes, you're always active. Where, if you're just waiting, waiting, for that one stage that suits you and then it doesn't pay off, or something happens leading up to it, or you make a mistake in the race, it's gone. That one opportunity is gone.'

It also made his fight against Kittel sustainable and more exciting.

But as Matthews stayed in touch with Kittel, who was leading the points classification, the man likened in appearance to Captain Ivan Drago began to feel the body blows and pay the price for his fast start. Kittel was four days away from reaching Paris when on stage 17 in the mountains he did what no rider wants to do at the Tour: abandon. Banged up from a crash, he dismounted his bike and waited for a team car to collect him, covering his face with his hands as photographers arrived like bees to a honey pot.

'On that day I was already not in my perfect condition any-more because I was the days before a bit sick, I had a stomach bug, and I couldn't eat well so I lost already a lot of energy,' Kittel recalls.

'I was feeling better on that day but just not good enough. And then the crash happened, which sort of really, you know, knocked my sore body in that moment and I couldn't really get into my rhythm anymore.'

The 183-kilometre stage from La Mure to Serre Chevalier was the second-last day in the mountains of the 2017 Tour. It featured four categorised climbs including two of the most difficult ascents – the Col de la Croix de Fer and the Col du Galibier. Primož Roglič took line honours.

The Col de la Croix de Fer, which stands 2067 metres above sea level, came just before the halfway mark of the stage, and Kittel crashed before it.

'It was just at the start of these big, big climbs,' he says.

'It was really a difficult moment to crash that early in the race and then when I had to continue, I immediately felt, "Okay, I can't really keep my speed."'

Two Quick-Step teammates, Julien Vermote and Fabio Sabatini, rallied around Kittel to climb the staggering Croix de Fer that ramped up and up and up.

'I knew that it's a hard climb, especially that steep part in between after that short downhill, and I really, really couldn't hold my speed anymore. I knew that this is going to be probably not enough for the rest of the day,' Kittel continues.

'When I reached the top, I was so exhausted, I was so empty.

I was already far behind still having Julien and Fabio with me. On top I said, "OK I think it's impossible, I can't continue, I'm done with it.'"

In his own words, the dream was over. 'It was a real struggle to make that decision because it's giving up a dream and you have to decide that while you are climbing uphill somewhere, you have to think about what you want to do now and that was really hard.

'When I stepped into the car I was really, really disappointed.'

Matthews the same day had made gains. He won the intermediate sprint, reducing his deficit on the points classification to only nine, and at the end of stage 17, after Kittel abandoned, assumed the green jersey, which he then kept.

'It suited me really well to be active every single day going for the intermediates, going for the finals,' Matthews says.

'And actually, the twenty-one days felt like it went over in a flash, attacking every single day rather than just sitting in the peloton being a number.

'Standing on the podium in Paris with the green jersey – that's pretty hard to beat.'

The competition for points classification is a slow burner, something that Bennett learned when he won it. Pure sprinters like Bennett had worn the green jersey for short periods during Sagan's reign – a stage or several days during a Tour – but no one had been able to keep it from Sagan's grasp until Bennett went head-to-head with him in 2020. Prior to then some pure sprinters, like Caleb Ewan, reckoned that the effort of sprinting to win intermediate primes, where Sagan and Matthews made inroads, would detract from their ability to claim stages.

'If I'm honest I was like every other sprinter that said it's too hard, it will take energy from my legs, when I first went in,' Bennett says.

The green jersey swapped between the shoulders of the pair multiple times before Bennett's victory on stage 10, hours before which I wrote a column saying Sagan would endure. That was unfortunate timing. The Irishman and his new Deceuninck–Quick-Step squad proceeded to force Sagan into a position that was somewhat foreign. Poitschke says that 2020 was the first year Sagan needed his whole team to work for him at the Tour.

'And we did, many times in the race; early action to drop Sam or take [on] the race hard and try everything to bring him in a good position,' says Poitschke.

'He fought so many years for that. He was mostly the strongest rider and could catch it.'

Sagan was disadvantaged when he was relegated on stage 11 for a bump on Belgian Wout van Aert but, unlike the incident years before with Cavendish, Poitschke took that one on the chin.

'Many times, he was too far away to win the green jersey,' Poitschke says.

'[2020] was the first time he was, I like to say, not on his best level. I mean, it was also a special season. He had a very long lockdown in Monaco that he really [can't] train there and that was not easy for him to prepare the first races as well. Then we saw in the Tour he's strong but not the ... strongest.'

Bennett's initial aim had been to collect points but not waste energy on the intermediates, an approach which gradually began to change.

'The first week I was there but I never really sprinted for

them, I just followed the wheels and [went] in the slipstream so I was collecting some points so that it wouldn't get away from me, but I wasn't taking a lot out of my legs,' he recalls.

The opportunity to get a photo with then teammate Julian Alaphilippe while the Frenchman was in the *maillot jaune* became a motivating factor.

'But then [there] came one point where it was like, "I'm really close here, it would be really nice to wear it for a day and it'd be a cool photo with Julian in yellow and me in green, it'd be a nice memory." And for sure I wouldn't win it,' Bennett continues.

'So, then I went for [it] that day and I was like, "This is nice." Then I lost it and then it kind of came back and I was like, "I want this now." I started chasing it.'

Bennett estimates that he could have claimed one or two more stages of the 2020 Tour had he not focused on the green jersey. But that was the choice he made.

'I was looking at the stages ahead in the race and I was like, "Right, I'm going to have to give up any other chances of the stage win for this green jersey because this opportunity might never come again and there is no better time than this moment, so we have to put everything into this." That was between stage ten and thirteen,' he explains.

'So, then we started to really focus on that and trying to win the intermediate sprints and trying to add up where I won't go for the sprints, where I would, because I knew he [Sagan] was going to get points on other days.

'All of a sudden, I was like, "Holy shit, I could actually win this!"'

It was a physically, and especially mentally, tough task.

The last week Bennett was averaging three to four hours sleep a night because he couldn't switch off.

'I did notice it is completely different to my normal style in a Grand Tour because normally I have just my competitors, the pure sprinters, and we just go for the sprints at the end of the race and then, okay, we still have to get over the mountains, which are hard, but there was that time where you could mentally switch off,' he says.

The battles at the intermediate primes or in the lead-up to them were fierce. Like Matthews in 2017, Bennett had to race harder in order to mark moves from Sagan or Italian Matteo Trentin from the gun to the first prime of any given stage.

'And that could last anywhere from five minutes to an hour,' Bennett says.

'I was full-on racing at the beginning to make sure he [Sagan] didn't get away in a break for the intermediate; then there was the intermediate sprint and then there was the finals. Some days it was like there was three parts to the race instead of just one, and then I was racing the green jersey guys and I was racing the pure sprinters, so there was two different types of competitors and it added up.'

Sagan also obviously played to his own strengths.

'We're a bit different and a bit different in how we race,' says Bennett. 'He is a better climber and he tried to make full use of that. We had to get points sometimes in different areas where we could.'

It took Bennett time to adjust to the new tactics, the greater number of rivals he suddenly had and the bigger workload. But as the race progressed his legs got better and on stage 19, he felt his best. Two days later on the Champs-Élysées Bennett won his career second Tour stage victory to finish ninety-six points clear ahead of Sagan in the green jersey contest.

'He won three world champs and [seven] green jerseys, I've only won one green jersey, so I'm not comparing myself to him,' says Bennett. 'He has won what he has won because he is that special, you know. But I'm just proud of getting my one green jersey and it's a moment I won't forget.'

Bennett's triumph with Deceuninck–Quick-Step wasn't a surprise to his former Bora–hansgrohe team, which he returned to in 2022. Yet, it was to the man himself.

He had won stages at the Giro d'Italia and the Vuelta a España before but not the Tour. The 2020 edition was his career third appearance and first in four years.

Bennett was in awe of Deceuninck–Quick-Step when he joined the team at the beginning of the 2020 season. He was not your archetypal sprinter. Bennett always came across as hard-working and humble. He saw himself as an underdog and was more likely to berate than talk himself up.

Quick-step was *the* sprint team, had housed many, true, brazen sprinting greats and had now backed him to become one of them.

The squad has a service course in Wevelgem, Belgium. Upstairs, near general manager Patrick Lefevere's office, are about ten historical bikes. The one Johan Museeuw won Paris–Roubaix on in 2002 is there, still caked in mud. One of Cavendish's bikes is part of the line-up. Two bikes Tony Martin won time trial world championships on are there. So too is Belgian Tom Boonen's 2007 green jersey and the last ever bike he won Paris–Roubaix on.

Bennett was taken aback when he saw it all.

'I walked into this room, and I was so intimidated,' he admits.

'I was like, "I'm in this position where they're expecting me to get these results or something." I was like, "How am I going to get any results that show that I'm worthy of this position?" I was in there and, like, "What have I got myself into? I'm out of my depth."'

'Six months later my bike, my green bike, [was] the first bike when you walk in.'

Bennett laughs nervously when I ask if Sagan said anything to him after the square beating.

'Ah.'

He falls silent.

'Yeah, he did.

'It was grand. To be fair, we all have a competitive nature and he congratulated me as well.'

Bennett adds, 'He's basically Mr Green, isn't he? He won it so many years in a row.

'If he wasn't there and I won green I don't think it would have been as special.

'It was a really enjoyable race, really competitive and I really enjoyed it. Regardless of the outcome, I really enjoyed the battle with him.'

Bennett was sidelined from the 2021 Tour due to injury and didn't get a chance to defend his title.

At the race, Sagan persevered for as long as he could, knowing his knee wasn't right after a crash involving Ewan on stage 3, but eventually abandoned. Ewan's first thought after the crash was about the green jersey, before he realised, he'd broken his collarbone in four places.

It left an opening for Cavendish to claim his career second

maillot vert, finishing thirty points ahead of Matthews. Just past the finish line in Paris, Cavendish and Matthews, in respectful acknowledgement of their fight against each other, hugged it out before finding their respective families and teammates.

I wondered. Had Bennett kicked off a movement that would see pure sprinters reclaim the jersey for a concerted period of time? Ewan had for many years ruled out a shot at green, but it was high on the agenda going into the 2021 Tour.

'I'd like to think so,' says Bennett.

'But you know the pure sprinters won when Peter wasn't really firing on all cylinders.'

He reasons that there are now not only more riders going for green, but a different calibre, a different generation again, pointing to the likes of Mathieu van der Poel, the twenty-seven-year-old who marked a stint in the yellow jersey at the 2021 Tour, and van Aert, who won a flat stage, a mountain stage and time trial stage at the same edition.

'We haven't seen van der Poel go for it, we haven't seen van Aert go for it, so that calibre of rider hasn't really gone for or succeeded in the last two years of going for the green jersey,' Bennett continues.

'I think for the moment it has sparked it again. It shows that it is doable, like, definitely not undoable.

'We have to see this year because I know van Aert is probably going for it, so that will make things difficult.'

CHAPTER 7
A SPRINTER'S MINDSET

Even in retirement, Robbie McEwen is as self-assured as great sprinters of the Tour de France are touted to be.

He's just been to a Bunnings hardware store having figured that he doesn't need to pay tradies a premium for fix-it jobs at home during the pandemic. He can do it himself for a fraction of the cost with the right equipment.

'I've fixed a TV, I replaced the power board, saved myself four hundred and fifty dollars with a one-hundred-and-six-dollar part. I've fixed a dishwasher; I replaced a little switch in it and the repair would have been, again, four hundred dollars is pretty standard, but I repaired it for fifty dollars. They're just little wins.'

McEwen knows a lot about winning. He won the green jersey three times, in 2002, 2004 and 2006. Part of why he was so successful at the Tour was his mentality. As a pre-eminent sprinter in a field loaded with equally capable fast men, he would tell rivals they had no chance of beating him.

'I can't remember who it was, but I remember saying to someone once, "There's no point in you being here." That was in the bunch in the final kilometres. "You're not racing to win, you're racing to get second, now piss off,"' McEwen says.

And whoever it was did.

'I think he thought to himself, "He's right." And I was right. I wasn't talking shit. I wasn't trying to trick him. It was just fact,' McEwen laughs.

The Queenslander is not daring tradies in the same way but his resolution from then to now remains the same. He's not just good at this DIY thing, he's great at it.

'I'm a flat-pack ninja. Piece of piss. I hate them, but I get them done really easy,' McEwen continues. 'Rule number one on flat packs is count every single part that you're supposed to have first. If you don't have every single bit, including the last little screw, don't even start.'

Stereotypes are born from truth and the common comparison of sprinters to boxers has merit in terms of mindset and physicality involved in the race to win.

'When it came to a sprint,' McEwen recalls, 'I would go in with a firm belief that I was the best one there and I will win, I should win, I shall win, and I will put myself in the best position and everybody else should resign themselves to the fact that that's where I'm going to be because that's where I should be.

'You believe that. You put that in your own head. And then the hope is it becomes a self-fulfilling prophecy.

'You think to yourself, "I'm the best, I've worked hard, I'm better than these other guys and I'm going to win."'

When McEwen's generation waned towards retirement it gave rise most notably to Mark Cavendish, who advertised his belief in himself on a greater scale. It became, until the arrival of Marcel Kittel, his commercial slogan: 'Fastest man on two wheels. Fact.'

In terms of physical appearance, Cavendish isn't an imposing figure, standing at 1.75m he looks from top to toe a bit like a hobbit but has the same air and gait as a boxer. In the early days of his career, he was uncompromising. The morning of the elite men's road race at the 2011 World Championships in Copenhagen, Denmark, which he won ahead of Australia's Matt Goss and German nemesis André Greipel, Cavendish had sent me a text message.

'See you on the podium,' it read.

His focus, as I've known it to be, and which he has waxed lyrically about, was to be not one of the best but the best ever. And everything from the way he positioned himself in a room, to his interactions with the media – one minute charming, the next confrontational – to how he competed and treated his closest rivals reinforced that power dynamic.

Cavendish's desire was to leave a legacy, which the Briton sealed at the 2021 Tour, equalling Eddy Merckx's all-time stage win record of thirty-four, in a comeback performance that was unfathomably lucky but still stirring and everlasting.

During that edition Cavendish had tried to convince the press he was a changed man. No longer the boy racer who was at times a self-described 'prick' but now a grown-up veteran. A fan video of him dressed in the green jersey screaming at a mechanic apparently over something to do with his bike at a stage start during the third week suggested otherwise. The 'twenty-year-old who wanted to fight the world' was still there.

He wasn't the best sprinter in cycling any more. He hadn't

been for a long time, but he was at that Tour.

Kittel recalls there being a general respect between himself and rivals during his reign, but such is the nature of the job that he equally wasn't inviting Cavendish or Greipel, his main competition, over for Sunday barbecues.

'I can really say my relationships with opponents was always good, but also never that close,' he says. 'In the end you are, everyone is, focused a bit on himself. I don't know if there can really be space to let a personal relationship develop. For me that wasn't the case, not much.'

Cavendish and then Kittel had been the personification of two generations. Sometimes they'd won a stage of the Tour before it had even begun.

Standing amid the peloton behind the start line at the Tour I'd ask their rivals: 'Can you beat Kittel today?' or 'Can you beat Cavendish today?'

In my experience, and except for Greipel, the answer was usually the same: 'It'll be hard to beat Kittel,' they'd say. 'It'll be hard to beat Cavendish.'

They may as well not have started.

Kittel shied away from talking about legacy, but his goal was in keeping with Cavendish's and others who had dominated before him.

'The mindset was basically to try to be the best in the world and try to beat the best at that time, most of all Cav and Greipel. That for me was my main ambition,' Kittel says.

'For other sprinters it's the same: you want to be better than the rest and it really is in the middle of your focus.

'Talking about my mentality, I tried to always give my best, to be focused, to try to make sure that everything is all right, that I have the right team around me, that I'm in shape, and then just motivate [myself] in the sprints with that thought of trying to beat everyone else and prove myself again and again and again.'

Kittel took early retirement in May 2019, after a season and a bit with Katusha where it was clear he wasn't happy. Cavendish hadn't won a stage at the Tour since 2016; tumbleweeds had replaced the once-heaving crowds that moved like a tidal wave outside his team bus. Two of his closest teammates, Australian lead-out specialist Mark Renshaw and Austrian Bernhard Eisel, retired in 2019 and 2020, respectively. Renshaw called time on his career partly because he was over enduring repeated kickings in a position he and Cavendish were traditionally not accustomed to – the back of the peloton.

A new generation had come to the fore and the sprint scene had changed once more, now again resembling something closer to what McEwen had faced.

There wasn't one sprinter clearly ahead of the rest, rather many, who were all of equal capability and standing. Among them was Caleb Ewan, Sam Bennett, Dylan Groenewegen and Fabio Jakobsen, Colombian Fernando Gaviria, German Pascal Ackermann, Italian Elia Viviani, and others became the story. It was their faces plastered on magazine covers, on yellow and black posters that decorated areas at the Tour.

None have been bold enough to promote themselves to pre-eminence yet.

'I think we have four or five guys that are really good and I'm one of the fastest,' says Groenewegen.

Predecessors described them as a different sort of hybrid, still quick but lither and more adept at climbing.

The tall, broad-shouldered Ackermann in a bunch sprint channels his intent in a different way to McEwen, for example. He's not telling Groenewegen, 'My wheel,' or undermining Ewan, for example, with fighting talk off the bike, a tactic that Cavendish employed against Greipel.

'I would say out of the race I'm a really nice guy but in the race I'm totally different,' Ackermann says.

'I don't like to speak in the race because if I have to race or if I have to go for the result, I'm really focused.'

Ackermann in the race is more of a silent assassin.

'I think sometimes I look [to] the other guys arrogant because I don't speak in the peloton, I just move up and speak nothing. It looks sometimes a bit bad, but I have to be concentrated in the race and that's my thing. Outside of the race I can have fun and do everything.'

Ewan has separated himself slightly from his contemporaries. Physically, he's shorter than them, built like McEwen, or Cavendish. And he places an emphasis on quality wins over quantity. He won fewer races than some of his rivals in 2019 but, as he noted, claimed two stages at the Giro d'Italia and the Tour, respectively. One of his main objectives for the 2021 season was to win stages at all three Grand Tours.

Ewan started well at the Giro, claiming two stages before leaving early to recover and then ready for the Tour, which was cut short.

Sprawled out on bitumen that had burned parts of his jersey off his back, McEwen didn't get a chance to see any of his teammates, who were talking to media past the finish line, before he was taken from where he crash-landed to hospital. Cavendish though circled back to them. 'Sorry guys,' he said with sympathy, recognising their great loss, which ultimately played to his advantage. Cavendish won his first of four stages the next day.

In all the times I've worked with Cavendish he has never, ever rated another sprinter above himself. Ever. So, when I asked him during the 2021 Tour what he made of his rivals his answer surprised me.

The field he competed against at the Tour wasn't full strength. Ewan crashed out, and the likes of Bennett, Gaviria, Groenewegen, Ackermann and Viviani weren't selected to compete. Gaviria tested positive twice for COVID-19 in 2020 so was building back up and trying to galvanise his UAE Emirates team around him, which took Tadej Pogačar to the Tour anyway. Groenewegen only returned in May from a nine-month ban following his involvement in a crash at the 2020 Tour of Poland where Jakobsen was injured and placed into a medically-induced coma.

I wanted to gauge with Cavendish if their collective absence had something to do with his mounting success at the Tour with Deceuninck–Quick-Step.

Cavendish had spent years trudging through a winless wilderness before he re-joined the team on a one-year deal in 2021.

You could in fact argue that had it not been for a television reporter who in 2020 plucked Cavendish out of an anonymous crowd at the finish of Gent-Wevelgem, which ran in October that year, giving him a mouthpiece to tearily contemplate retirement through want of a contract, his career could have ended with a literal, wet-eyed whimper, not befitting his brash nature or body of work, built on passion and ferocity.

Cavendish gave due credit to the Tour field. Second-tier team Alpecin-Fenix won a stage with Belgian Tim Merlier and then backed Jasper Philipsen, who was always in the mix with a lead-out that, I think, given a bit more time to gel, will become a force. But then Cavendish singled out the departed Ewan.

'He's the one I see that he can really think and play out a sprint. He's small, he jumps from wheel to wheel and he's the one, since he was a kid, I've been a fan of his,' Cavendish said.

He related to Ewan.

'I really, really wanted,' Cavendish continued, 'just for an honour, to be able to sprint head-to-head with him and I think that would have been beautiful for the Tour de France as well.'

My colleagues thought it was a commercially savvy answer. Refer to an Australian rider when you're speaking to an Australian journalist and you're more likely to get airtime in Australia. And he is commerically savvy. But it was the closest I'd heard Cavendish come to recognising someone equal to, if not above, him. To be the best you must compete against the best.

It is how Cavendish has come to measure his own performances. His showing at the 2021 Tour bought him another twelve-month deal at Quick-Step but when he started his 2022 season at the Tour of Oman, he refused to talk about the Tour de France.

'I think everybody coming into the new season looks forward to starting the season to see their shape. You don't really know. It doesn't matter how you're going until you compare yourself with the other people,' Cavendish said.

The call not to speak about the Tour contributed to a narrative that pit him up against teammate Jakobsen for selection.

But it was also, going on his measure, understandable.

At the beginning of the 2022 season every marquee pure sprinter was back – from injury, adversity, obscurity and many had also changed teams. Powerhouses Jakobsen and Groenewegen got wins on the board early. So too did Ewan, Viviani and Gaviria, who are more versatile. Cavendish also chalked one, but younger rivals believed it was his experience rather than speed that would keep him in the mix. Even in March though none really knew where they stood in comparison to each other.

Ewan has drawn comparison to Cavendish since he was a young gun competing on the domestic circuit in Australia. He won a stage of the Bay Crits criterium series in Victoria as a teenager with a low, aerodynamic position uncannily like that of the tempestuous champion he grew up watching on TV.

But, after his crash in 2021, Ewan was forced to watch the Tour from his home in Monaco and seeing Cavendish on the TV this time was not an inspiring experience. Many riders who have been in that position – viewing a race they are normally a huge part of – don't like talking about it. Some can't even watch.

'The stage I crashed I was pretty much in a position to win, and I felt good,' Ewan recalls. 'I don't know if I would have won but I was definitely going to be close enough to winning, and then there were a lot of stages that really suited me.'

He continues, 'I could have done much more than crash out on stage three.

'I wish actually that, if I was going to crash, I would crash after the first few sprint stages and then at least maybe I could have won something and got something out of the Tour.

'It's disappointing when you get nothing out of it. In the end, I got nothing out of it. It's a whole year's work for nothing.'

Despite a desperate bid to be fit for the ensuing Vuelta a España, Ewan didn't make it. He lined up for the World Championships instead, mentally exhausted and looking forward to a holiday.

'To be honest I would have loved to have sprinted against Cav as well,' Ewan says.

'A sprinter that I grew up watching and admiring, it would have been really cool to go head-to-head with him at a Tour de France. I'm a bit disappointed that it didn't work out in the end.'

The problem with the boxer stereotype about sprinters is that it inaccurately portrays them as one-dimensional machines void of emotions outside of brute aggression.

The flipside of overt confidence is insecurity, which none of them are above, especially at the Tour.

'It's the one race as a sprinter where you can actually make your career,' says McEwen. 'You could literally not line up in another race but if you went to the Tour every year and won one or two stages, and a green jersey every now and again, you'd make your entire career on it. You wouldn't have to ride a single other race.'

When Ewan reflected on his Tour debut at the end of the 2019 season, he described the pressure and stress he shouldered at that edition as unhealthy. On a personal level, Ewan left for the race before his first child, born premature, was discharged from hospital.

Professionally, there were numerous pressures that added to the serious expectation he shouldered. Pundits, at least in Australian circles, had hyped up Ewan and his ability to compete at the Tour since he was seventeen.

'My Tour de France debut has been spoken about probably almost since I first ever won Bay Crits,' he recalled to me in October that year.

'Even from then, people always, not that I deserved to have people talking about me going to the Tour de France at that point, but people always just jumped to I think the biggest conclusion.'

He continued, 'Then you have the media and always the question. I saw heaps of people getting asked the question, more experienced people like riders, coaches, "Do they think that I'll be able to go to the Tour de France and win?" and this is already when I was still a teenager.'

Ewan was meant to debut at the Tour in 2018 before his then Mitchelton-Scott team famously reneged on the selection. The surprise snub made in the name of 'development' added to the attention he received when he finally did take to the start line just days before his twenty-fifth birthday with new team Lotto–Soudal.

At Lotto–Soudal Ewan also replaced Greipel as the team's No. 1 sprinter. Greipel was one of the best sprinters ever. Up until his retirement at the end of 2021 he was competitive, and the most winning active rider ahead of Cavendish.

He had offered to work for Ewan in 2019 but the Australian politely declined and Greipel transferred teams.

'When I was signing with the team it was something that the team spoke about and I was happy for him to stay, he is someone that I could have learned a lot from,' Ewan recalled then.

'But in that sense as well he's not a lead-out man, he's a sprinter. Sprinters don't change like that. Sprinters don't go from being one of the best sprinters in the world to next year,

"Oh I want to lead-out this young guy who is coming to the team," when he's been the main guy of the team for so long.'

Ewan continued, 'I think the team almost needed with the changeover from André to me, I think the team needed a clear cut. It was like a whole new team was beginning. Their plan with me is probably to do the same as with André, and go a long time with the team, develop with the team.'

Greipel during his long tenure at Lotto inspired many teammates to work for him and developed a loyal lead-out train, including Adam Hansen, Jens Debusschere, compatriot Marcel Sieberg, Greg Henderson, and others, which rarely changed.

Hansen once said Greipel's Achilles heel was confidence. That was not necessarily in bunch kicks. If Greipel had open road ahead of him, he was usually golden. But a critical question from the press, for example, could plant a seed of doubt that could sprout into an impenetrable forest. Towards the end of his tenure with Lotto, on a bad day, Greipel would avoid post-race interviews. I assumed this was to minimise this risk.

In contrast to some of the other sprinters, before his breakthrough win at the 2020 Tour with Deceuninck–Quick-Step, Bennett was never bullish.

'I was always used to being the underdog, I always came in kind of a little bit off the radar. There was no pressure, and I came from behind to win,' he says. 'I always judged my sprint off somebody else's train or had somebody else as a point of reference.'

At and in the lead-up to the 2020 Tour though, he became a reference point and rivals would judge their position and timing off his wheel.

'That was a lot of pressure and that took a little bit of time to get used to, and because we're in this time that any little mistake, there's five or six guys that are going to take the opportunity that are right behind you,' he explains.

'I'm used to it now and I don't even think about it anymore. But, initially, that was a big change, and it was something I think I had to get stronger for, kind of train a little different. It was a different approach to sprinting than I was used to, but I've adapted.'

Even Cavendish at the beginning of the 2021 Tour appeared to be uncharacteristically unsure of himself.

The Tour Cavendish was once synonymous with had also become a little foreign. He didn't complete the 2016 or the 2017 editions and, during his last start, in 2018, he finished outside of the time limit on stage 11. His team then, Dimension Data, didn't select him to compete in 2019, nor did his next stable, Bahrain-Merida, in 2020.

At the beginning of the 2021 Tour, away from the TV cameras, Cavendish was sensitive. He wasn't comfortable talking about expectation, throwing shade at one journalist who raised the Merckx record he was then four stages off from equalling.

However, as he started winning again, his answers became more robust; he was friendlier and well-mannered, at press conferences done via video link-up. He was having fun again, amply supported by the best team in the business, and it showed.

Patrick Lefevere's gamble on signing him had paid off.

'Always I say you're allowed one mistake a year, and it wasn't a mistake,' Lefevere says.

The Belgian cycling stalwart was standing outside the team bus following Cavendish's first stage win of the campaign and thirty-first of his career. His eyes watered not from emotion but age as I asked him, then sixty-six, for an interview in English.

I don't know Lefevere that well and, in fact, after the Tour publicly critcised him.

Bennett had broken his contract with Bora–hansgrohe in order to join Lefevere's outfit. When it was announced, days before the 2021 Tour, that Cavendish would substitute him in the race many were shocked. Bennett had enjoyed a cracking start to the season. It was known that he'd injured his knee during a training in the lead-up to the Tour.

'The chain slipped and I hit my knee off the handlebar. It was something pretty simple,' he says.

But the general assumption was that he'd be back in time for the race.

'You build your whole career up to that point, when you're at your peak, and then something so silly takes that opportunity away from you, so I couldn't watch it,' he recalls.

Lefevere during the Tour questioned the severity of Bennett's injury and his honesty around the situation.

When Bennett at the mid-point of the season considered his options and signed with Bora–hansgrohe, which now wasn't laden with stars competing for the same spots at races, Lefevere compared it to 'women who return home after domestic abuse'.

Waiting for the triumphant Cavendish to return, Lefevere with his silver-grey hair, a face mask covering his nose and mouth, briefly contemplated me, and then obliged to do the interview.

'Being here for him is already the best thing he could have because eight months ago he was not a rider anymore,' Lefevere says.

If anyone knows the mindset of a sprinter it's Lefevere. Bennett, Cavendish, Kittel, Gaviria and Viviani have all spearheaded his team in the last ten years. His experience goes well beyond that though.

I ask him if Cavendish is the best sprinter he has worked with.

'He's probably one of the best, certainly at this age, but it's very unfair to say this because I worked with Mario Cipollini, he was the first sprinter I worked with,' Lefevere says contemplatively.

'And Tom Steels, nine stages in the Tour. Kittel was very, very fast.'

Lefevere, leaning against a metal barricade separating us, then circles back.

'Numbers don't lie. If you win thirty-one stages in the Tour, it means something.'

All sprinters want to be the best; they all want to win. But their degree of conviction, and how they are able to achieve their success, differs.

'My main advantage over my rivals was my speed combined with my ability to hold it for a long time,' says Kittel.

'I could really push high watts with a high cadence for a long time. On the other side, that was my weakness. I wasn't able to kick like someone like Caleb Ewan or Mark Cavendish. I could build up speed over a longer period but [was] a bit slower than the top sprinters like Mark, or Caleb.'

Lefevere says versatility and the nerve to take risks while

riding at up to 70 kilometres an hour in a bunch sprint finale also plays into it.

So too does visualisation for some riders. Ewan is best when he can see the finish a few times before he contests it. It's why he's good at criteriums, he says.

Cavendish also has a strong recall. Before my first Tour in 2012 I'd interviewed him about the final stage in Paris, which that year I ended up canvassing on the back of a motorbike.

As my driver and I accelerated closer and closer towards the Champs-Élysées finishing circuit, Cavendish's voice entered my head like commentary. Turn for turn, his description of the run-in was flawless.

Bunch sprints at the Tour, like the riders who contest them, are often described in aggressive, chaotic terms.

'Of course, there are moments in the sprint where you give an elbow, where it's just your job, you are trying to go for a victory,' Kittel says.

But there is another element. One that isn't routinely described.

Navigating the sprints and winning also comes down to being able to think clearly and react at the same time.

Bennett's first stage victory at the 2020 Tour was emotionally charged but his second on the Champs-Élysées eleven days later was not so much.

'Coming from the last corner to the finish line on the Champs-Élysées, it felt like it was six minutes long even though it was only twenty seconds or thirty seconds or something,' he says.

'Everything just, I know it sounds cheesy, excuse my language, it sounds cheesy as fuck, but do you know, like, if you're watching a movie and everything just slows down, everything goes silent, so you hear your heart beating.' He laughs. 'It was like that!

'I was in the zone. Every decision I made was clear. I knew who was where, the timing and everything. It was just one of my most enjoyable memories and, like, best ever result. It was a super special moment.'

CHAPTER 8
GAME CHANGERS

Great sprinters, to thrive at the Tour de France, no matter how good they are, need people in their corner.

At the 2021 Tour, Mark Cavendish, at thirty-six, relied on his lead-out train arguably more than any other year. The finish line of the final stage on the Champs-Élysées, which offered him a chance to eclipse Eddy Merckx's record, was 300 metres further up the road than usual and Cavendish lost contact with his teammates and got boxed in, finishing third behind Wout van Aert and Jasper Philipsen.

Flat stages in which pure sprinters compete for victories are often described as boring because the script is familiar. A breakaway goes up the road and the peloton, minutes behind them, rides tempo until it decides to ready for the finish and reign in the escapees with anywhere from say 30 to 10 kilometres of the stage remaining.

It is a bit like cruising for most of the day but with the knowledge you have a crucial exam to sit at 5 pm. For some the lead-up to the exam is boring, for others it's a tense exercise where they must maintain their self-belief.

Each sprinter has a lead-out train that forms in front of them, single file, to help position and bring them up to speed as the finish line nears. Ideally, the sprinter will be protected and kept out of the wind until they launch with about 200 to 250 metres remaining. Then, the rest is on them.

At high speed the sprinters and their teams must maintain focus and communicate as they bump shoulders, handlebars, and, in the most aggressive of situations, butt heads with rivals also thundering along for pole position.

Teammates look for and shout instructions at each other over the whir of fast spinning wheels and gears clicking.

The sprinters themselves concentrate on the tyre imme-diately in front of theirs to help navigate through the unyielding pack. That wheel is preferably a teammate's but if they get lost or something in their lead-out doesn't work then another. They'll look for gaps to squeeze through, any clean path to the line.

British time trial specialist Alex Dowsett has spent most of his career riding for teams focused on the general classification. When he transferred to Katusha in 2018 and was assigned to Marcel Kittel's sprint train the adjustment of being competitive in bunch kicks as opposed to taking a back seat went against his nature.

'I've made a lot more enemies than in previous years,' he told me then. 'You are trying to ride people off wheels, jostle for position quite aggressively. I'm like banging handlebars and sort of in my head going, "Sorry, sorry, sorry."'

When Cavendish won stage 13 of the 2021 Tour de France

to equal Merckx's all-time stage win record the immediate reaction in the press room was not solely in response to his historic sprint but also the effort of his teammate Michael Mørkøv.

The Dane was so strong he finished second on the line in the ancient, fortified city of Carcassonne.

Deceuninck–Quick-Step team manager Patrick Lefevere says great sprinters can win with and without a lead-out. Despite this, he has procured the best sprint train there currently is.

When Sam Bennett was appointed as the spearhead of that train in 2020, he initially felt intimidated. It took time to adjust and gel with the support riders at his disposal but there was never a question about winning.

'The way they run there's real confidence, you're just reassured that everything you're doing is correct and you just go in knowing what to do,' says Bennett.

'I feel myself actually that it wasn't until the Tour where we had intermediate sprints and sprint finishes, because it was a weird year [2020] in general, that it took until the Tour de France where all the sprints ended up being more practised and more practised and then it just clicked.

'They have such a strong foundation with the riders that like to support riders – and that's just the support riders,' Bennett continues.

'Like, everybody has a job to do in the win and everybody is proud of what they contribute. The morale is just so high, and it fuels itself. I think, also, once it gathers momentum it keeps going and it's contagious in the team. It spreads and grows.'

Lefevere is right in saying sprinters can win without lead-outs.

Bennett says that during his stint with Quick-Step there was never a definite plan going into flat stages, even though he trusted Mørkøv and others to pilot him successfully.

'In the final metres I have to also make sure that I make the right decision too,' he says.

It takes the pressure off Bennett knowing he can trust his teammates and that they'll invariably be in the right place, at the right time, when he needs them.

'But to be honest, I don't really mind whether I have to chase somebody or go first or whatever, I like that I'm really versatile in that way. I like to be able to go in and race, if that makes sense,' he says.

The reward for those who work for champion sprinters is that when their leaders win, they've been a part of something great. Some even do rise to notoriety. Mark Renshaw, who plans to write his own book, spent years supporting Cavendish and became known as the best lead-out specialist in the business.

One of the most iconic photos of the Tour is that of Renshaw holding on to finish second behind Cavendish on the final stage of the 2009 edition. It was a picture-perfect one-two on the Champs-Élysées, both men in frame with arms aloft in celebration.

The pair competed with the same rigour. Renshaw was famously booted from the 2010 Tour for headbutting rival lead-out man Julian Dean, who was working for Tyler Farrar. But Renshaw and Cavendish were different people, as the chief and deputy in cycling often are.

Cavendish and Mørkøv only had a short time to gel before the 2021 Tour but in press conferences Cavendish chose not to highlight this and instead placed emphasis on personality.

'He doesn't get the banter, well, he gets it, but he's not interested, he just tells me to shut up,' Cavendish observed.

'That's why he's a good lead-out man. As it was with Mark Renshaw, he's an anti-me in that he stays cool, calm, does the job and that's incredible to follow.'

Despite the recognition, there's still a thankless element to the selfless task of being a lead-out man, or support rider in general.

Sprinters are a meticulous bunch and can be blunt. While they are quick to thank their teammates profusely in post-race interviews when everything goes right, they also often hold those supporting them accountable when a plan doesn't come together.

In the rare moments Caleb Ewan is off the pace, he has sometimes unabashedly pointed to a failing in his lead-out, rather than his own error. A good lead-out, Ewan says, guarantees consistency more so than when a rider is freestyling, jumping from wheel to wheel where the chances of getting boxed in or crashing are greater.

'If you have a lead-out where you're not really having to fight with other riders, fight for a wheel, then the chance of winning is a lot higher,' he says.

'It's definitely something I'm working on. We're maybe missing one or two guys in our lead-out. There's only so much that Roger [Kluge] and Jasper [De Buyst] can do when you're going up against stronger lead-outs, but the team is really committed to getting more guys in and really strengthening the lead-out. If we can get something that's similar to what Quick-Step has then I can win a bit more.'

Deceuninck–Quick-Step were imperative to Cavendish's success at the 2021 Tour, and he acknowledged that.

When questioned about his mindset, what gave him an edge at that edition, he was momentarily confused and then had just two words: 'My team.'

'Everybody wants to come here,' Lefevere says, 'and the guys who left the team want to come back. It means we have something, sprinting in our body and our blood.'

Deceuninck–Quick-Step recognised Cavendish's strengths and shortfalls at the 2021 Tour – that he didn't have as much puff compared to his younger years, for example – and worked with that, ensuring, where possible, that he did the least amount of work before a sprint and kicked as late as possible.

That is what lead-outs are designed for, but Deceuninck–Quick-Step took it to another level. On stage 10 Cavendish still had a teammate steering him with 150 metres remaining, having earlier been at the front and sheltered on the approach to the finish.

'I remember buying cycling magazines when I was younger,' Cavendish reflected after the stage, when I asked him to talk about his lead-out, 'and it was like, "the art of sprinting" and stuff. They'd write a textbook of how a lead-out works, and today was a case study in that. Once we lined up, it's about not necessarily going full gas but keeping control and going full gas when you need to. I can honestly say I'm humbled. It's about delivering each rider to their best place possible and that's what they do here and that's ultimately why this team is successful.'

In the mountains the team would surround him in the *grupetto*, as they did Bennett the year before, and help haul him up within the time limit. On some of those days Cavendish would cross the line, climb off his bike, and hug his teammates, who were no more suited to the ascents than him, as if he'd won.

In some ways he had. Robbie McEwen compares the stages in the mountains to literal torture.

'As a sprinter, you suffer a lot more in the Tour to finish it compared to a climber because you're not suited to the course like they are,' he says.

'When you got in the mountain stages, and they were just, you know, one after the other, and then you got through the mountains and had two medium mountain stages, say in the Massif Central, it was horrific.

'I don't know what you could do to suffer more, outside of proper torture.

'I sometimes thought to myself getting waterboarded would be easier than what I'm doing at that moment.'

Today there is no singular sprinter of reference but there is a lead-out train of reference and Mørkøv, despite beginning his Tour career in 2012 working for climbers including Alberto Contador, has become the key cog in that locomotive.

Mørkøv has a background in track cycling, which culminated with a gold medal in the Madison at the Tokyo Olympic Games. This background made his transition from being part of a general classification team at the Tour to racing for sprinters easier. In 2016 Norwegian big man Alexander Kristoff asked Mørkøv to come work for him at Katusha and Mørkøv changed his approach to pro cycling thereafter.

'When I joined Katusha with Kristoff, who was really having his best seasons at that time, I really put a lot of study into learning how to do the lead-outs, study how other guys did it, what was needed, what was the task,' he says. 'From there, I developed into it.'

Mørkøv, in six Tours, has only once ridden for himself, on debut in 2012 with team Saxo Bank–Tinkoff Bank when Contador was serving a doping suspension. A senior teammate emphasised to Mørkøv that he had a rare opportunity that season to do his own thing at the Tour and to make the most of it, which he did. Mørkøv marked a stint in the polka dot jersey, getting into breakaways and generally attacking. Thereafter though, his teammate's words proved accurate.

'I had to accept at one point it was not me who was able to win stages of the Tour de France or in the big races, the big classics, but my ambition was to win these big races,' he says.

'So, I realised and accepted that if I want to be a part of winning stages in the Tour it's not going to be for me but for a team member.

'I have the ambition to win the biggest races, I'm just realistic to know I don't have the level myself. So, what really motivates me is to pair up with a guy who can do it and give him that final touch to make him win.'

Mørkøv mirrored Bennett's race program in the lead-up to the 2020 Tour and through that became confident the Irishman would always be in position, on his wheel ready to launch.

He and Cavendish had only worked together three times in the lead-up to the 2021 Tour at two one-day races – Scheldeprijs in April and Elfstedenronde in June, then the Belgium Tour a week later. The difference in practise, through racing, was slight but significant at Elfstedenronde.

'All the way into the sprint we were in a perfect position,' Mørkøv recalls.

'Unfortunately, he lost my wheel around the last corner and from there we didn't manage to do a lead-out, so he finished very close to first place on second spot.

'If he would just have been that one bike length further ahead on my wheel, I think it could have been a different result.'

Results mean as much to support riders as they do to top sprinters. Renshaw once said there was no such thing as runner-up, just the winner and 'first loser'.

Mørkøv feels big pressure coming into a bunch kick and it can make him nervous, knowing he has a sprinter behind him, who is trusting his every move. A lack of trust can be an undoing in bunch sprints. If a sprinter doesn't gel with, or can't rely on, their lead-out they're at an immediate disadvantage. Conversely, if a sprinter can't stay on the wheels of whoever is in their lead-out then the task becomes harder for the team, having to first find their leader and then manoeuvre them into position.

'I embrace that. That's also why you're in the game,' Mørkøv says.

Trust, timing and execution are the foundations of a successful sprint train, and each prolific sprinter Mørkøv has worked with has been unique, in personality, strengths and weaknesses.

'They all have to be approached differently,' he says.

'I find it extremely motivating if I can be the game changer for that top sprinter, to make him win more than he would have done without me.'

And the game changers are invaluable to top sprinters when and if they click.

Renshaw and Bernhard Eisel were largely a package deal

when it came to Cavendish's contract talks and transferring teams. Bennett took Shane Archbold with him to Deceuninck–Quick-Step and then back to Bora–hansgrohe. Fernando Gaviria persuaded Max Richeze, who he likens to a 'big brother', to join him at UAE Emirates. Kluge followed Ewan from Mitchelton-Scott to Lotto–Soudal.

Good lead-out men become not only trusted pilots but confidants.

André Greipel's teammates at Lotto–Soudal propped him up when he needed a confidence boost, not just on the road.

'We were just a bunch of friends who got along really good and understood each other,' says Greipel's former teammate Jens Debusschere.

'In the most difficult times sometimes we were yelling at each other and angry at each other, but that's also part of the game.

'I think, especially when you feel you really have a shot with André, you really want to give everything for him because you know, eventually, he will win at least one stage.

'That was pushing all of us to a higher level than we were used to.'

The opposite can happen when that faith in a sprinter winning big starts to wane. Losses can have a reverberating effect through the whole team, which then gives less.

'The racing is so tough, both in a physical and mental way, that you really need to have a good connection to whoever you help,' Mørkøv says. 'You really want to give yourself one hundred and ten per cent for that guy, or for your team.

'I'm quite sure it would be hard to get it to work out if you for some reason didn't like the guy that you helped. But I also think when you pair up with someone you have to know them. You realise that you have to come along so you also try to come along.'

How quickly Deceuninck–Quick-Step pull that together each season, no matter which sprinter it is for, is truly remarkable because it's usually not something that happens overnight. It can take months, maybe even years, to get a lead-out train to gel, and sometimes it never does.

Kittel, during his seventeen-month tenure at Katusha, couldn't find the right formula and when his remonstrative post-race debriefs with teammates in full public view became more frequent than his general cheery countenance, it went hand in hand with declining results.

'I actually believe that the biggest part of preparation is not only happening in the months before but really in the years before that,' says Kittel. 'I mean, when I look at my career it took us, in the end, from 2011 until 2013 to be successful in the Tour de France, to be ready for it as a team as well, and I think that makes this combination to be the best sprinter quite difficult.

'You need to be in a good condition, but you also need to have a good team to support you,' he continues. 'And I think to build that up is a lot of work, is a lot of communication, racing together, training together and of course everything that is involved in terms of sacrifices with that – being away from home, crashing, suffering. That's all part of it.'

He goes on to say, 'I think I'm now known also as someone who was really focused on that, as working as a team and having a good team atmosphere around me. And you could see that in my results when that wasn't [the case].

'That was my strength and also at the same time my weakness, if I hadn't the team around me that I needed.'

Kittel was quick and also had the ability to sprint from a long way back and win a bike race, but he never underestimated the importance of his teammates.

'I needed my teammates to support me in the final, to help me there and in the end also to, in that way, help me to win the race,' he continues.

'That's also why I always said that for me cycling *is* a team sport, and they were really, really important. Everyone had his job, and you could see that in the results if that job was done well or not.'

Ewan hadn't even finished his 2021 season when he was voicing ways to improve his sprint train to reckon with Deceuninck–Quick-Step the next year.

'We have to use our guys a little bit too early and then in the last kilometre I'm by myself, the manpower is not there,' he says.

'With a few more guys that problem can be fixed. We have good guys, we just have to use them a bit too early whereas if we can use, say, Jasper, if he can do his job from four hundred metres to go then that's perfect but if he has to do his job going into the last kilometre then I'm left by myself for the last kilometre.

'It's definitely going to be stronger,' Ewan continues with resolve. 'It might take a bit of time to gel, but we have a few smaller races at the start of the year to get everything sorted.'

Like Mørkøv, a lot of lead-out riders will say that they committed to the position because they realised that they themselves weren't strong enough or ruthless enough or fast enough to vie for their own victories. Renshaw left Cavendish's service and changed teams for a stint to have a concerted go at chasing his own victories as a marquee sprinter but was never fully supported in that endeavour and later resumed his post.

When Debusschere joined Katusha and became the designated sprint leader at the 2019 Tour in lieu of Kittel's early retirement he appreciated the distinction between those two roles even more.

Like Mørkøv's debut in 2012, it was the only time the Belgian has ever been afforded an opportunity to race for himself at the Tour.

'Two weeks before the Tour, they told me, "You are our sprinter and no pressure, no stress, but we count on you to get some small results in the bunch sprints."'

No pressure on the biggest stage in a role you're not accustomed to and in a team that Mørkøv, in his time with the formerly Russian-registered squad, knew to be factional – the Russians would keep to themselves in one corner, the Spaniards in another, with the international riders figuring out a place in-between.

'I always knew well enough that I'm not a world class sprinter and I would never, or never say never, but I wouldn't win a bunch sprint at the Tour de France,' Debusschere continues.

'Normally I had my finish line in-between one kilometre and five hundred metres or four hundred metres [to go], the best-case scenario was four hundred metres, but if it was a little bit earlier it was not a problem.'

As Katusha's lead sprinter at that edition though, his finish line became the finish line, and there was a noted difference in performance levels.

'The pace, I can tell you, is really getting a lot higher in the last five hundred metres than before,' he says. 'To have still the kick, after already suffering for four to five kilometres on a really high pace, I could hold this pace or accelerate a little bit more but not have a super hard kick like the world class sprinters. This was a really big difference actually.'

Lead-out specialists diverge from sprinters in that they recognise they are not at the same level as those they serve, but equally they are assertive about their strengths and standing within their designated roles.

'You need to be quick to start a sprint when the speed is already high,' says Mørkøv.

'You don't need to be as quick as the quickest sprinters, but you need to be quite close to be able.

'It's important to have a good general level so you are as fresh as possible in the final to make the right decisions.'

Skills, experience and being open to learning also helps, especially in a field that is constantly evolving.

'You see young guys who come across who definitely have the power, the speed and the will to perform,' says Mørkøv. 'But they will be caught out many times in a bunch sprint because they make mistakes, like going too early, going to the wrong side, they box themselves in.'

You may not have heard about the men behind the Tour's champions but, as the saying goes, it takes an army to wage battle and win war.

CHAPTER 9
WHICH DIRECTION?

My eyes instinctively close shut as the wide roads flanked by vibrant sunflower fields give way to grass and then the stone outskirts of a village, which we're fast approaching.

I'm on a motorbike and I trust my driver Gaëtan implicitly; I've been his passenger before and know he's a pro when it comes to manoeuvring in the convoy at the Tour de France, which isn't for the faint-hearted.

It's as close as I'm going to get to the Tour de France without riding in the peloton myself.

My arms, which had been hanging loose by my sides, are now tense, my knuckles turning white as I grip the passenger handles by the seat.

As I open my eyes there is a team car to my right, so close that if I extended my knee out even slightly, I'd hit it.

The people inside don't seem to register that I'm there.

The windows of the car are all up. One sports director is driving, and another is sitting in the passenger seat with a computer tablet in their hands. In the back is a mechanic, his arm over spare wheels that have taken up the remaining space in the sedan. Spare bikes are firmly attached to the roof of the vehicle as it pushes ahead of us, closer to the village.

The sound of idling engines has given way to the roar of fast accelerations, and then abrupt braking. My ears start to ring as the tooting of car horns is drowned out by the five or six helicopters now circling above us to broadcast the race.

I look ahead to see the single lane entry into the village the peloton is passing through, under bunting that is zigzagging from rooftop to rooftop across the town.

My driver weaves in and out around the convoy, which now resembles a rally car race more than a procession.

The lane doesn't seem big enough for one sedan, let alone two.

'Brake, brake, brake!'

Was it by magic? Somehow everyone is in and through. Can the sedans retract to go through the impossible, like that double-decker bus for wizards in Harry Potter?

There are thousands of fans lining the road, which has widened again out the other side of the village. I lift my visor to rub my eyes and can smell sweet crepes in the air.

The fans cheer and wave at me like I'm a competitor and I feel obliged to wave back.

Some of them hold signs for home heroes Julian Alaphilippe and Romain Bardet. Others have national flags – from Colombia to Slovakia and Australia – which catch the wind.

The majority aren't there for one person though, or one team. They're applauding with respect and admiration for the entire race; the moving circus that, in a few short minutes, has come and gone.

My driver signals to me, asking if I want to catch up to the peloton and we accelerate ahead.

I spot some silver glittery things fanning across the road and can't make out what they are.

We brake again behind a bottleneck of riders.

There's been a crash in the drop-off zone, where riders can dump litter. The glittery things are caffeine gel and bar wrappers that have been discarded.

Most of the riders have cleared off, held up but not involved in the stack that brought a few down. I look back as we pass to see one, Luke Durbridge, limping around his bike, waiting for his team car to catch up and give him a spare.

The peloton has splintered now and, with the convoy behind us, I hear the familiar whir of wheels and clicking of gears. I turn my head to the side, not realising I am five seconds away from Dan Martin's face. But the Irish rider, like the sports directors in the convoy, doesn't seem to have clocked I'm there either. His eyes are focused forward, staring at what's ahead as the dust from the road kicks up around us.

The voice of cycling isn't commentator Phil Liggett, it's a Frenchman called Seb Piquet whose race updates crackle over the radios fitted to all vehicles in the convoy.

He's calling out the time gaps from the main group to the breakaway, then reading out the race numbers of the people in the escape.

Piquet is the Radio Tour speaker and everyone in the convoy responds to the information he provides. Sports directors, on a different frequency, can then pass that on to their riders, who all have a headphone taped into one ear.

'You have to be concentrated on what goes on all the time. And I mean all the time because something can happen at any moment – a crash, a rider asking for a bottle or whatever,' Piquet says.

He rides shotgun in a red car that follows the peloton on every stage. During the race he relies on scouts on motorbikes to tell him what he can't see in the breakaway, and time gaps to it and the bunch.

'The things I'll see on the Tour or other races are mostly the riders being dropped,' Piquet says. 'Often when you're watching your TV you see what the camera wants to show you and the camera is often at the front of the race.

'I'm at the back and I can see the guys struggling, I can see who is dropped, so that's also information I tend to give as much as possible – "Rider No. 131 dropped," and give all that information because that's not necessarily on your screen.'

Piquet works off many radio frequencies but the one I hear is the same as the team cars in the convoy.

If a rider needs to speak to their director, they might drop to the back of the peloton and raise their arm to signal that to Piquet.

'Movistar for rider one hundred and eighteen,' he will say.

He'll notify everyone of an incident, in English and then in French.

'Crash, crash.'

Then, as fast as possible, Piquet will name the teams impacted so their sports directors can speed up to the crash site and help the affected rider or riders.

At the beginning of every stage Piquet will list over the radio the number of riders who are starting and note if anyone has withdrawn overnight or that morning. At the end of every stage, he'll call the result.

'I have a big responsibility because I'm not allowed to fuck up,' Piquet says.

'If I say something wrong it will have repercussions.

'To give you an example, I don't know what stage it was, but it was a sprint stage on the Tour and with a kilometre to go there was a crash. Someone in the car, I won't name him, [said], "Phwoar, Cavendish is on the ground." And I didn't check.

'I immediately said, "Crash, Cavendish caught in the crash." And a kilometre later he was winning the stage.'

It's a mistake Piquet vowed never to make again.

'I'd rather not say anything than say something wrong. And also, don't trust anyone. If someone tells you Cavendish crashed, you want to see Cavendish on the floor before you call it.'

Piquet's updates are only part of a myriad of information sports directors like BikeExchange's Matt White process and act on, while instructing and encouraging the riders they drive behind every day.

Being a sports director, or DS, is one of the most significant occupations at the Tour, but a role White hadn't considered before his colleague and friend David Millar put it to him in the spring of 2007.

'The sport was in a bad place at the time, it was a pretty toxic environment, really, in professional cycling,' White recalls.

It was two years after Lance Armstrong won his seventh and

final Tour title in 2005. Records now read 'no winner'.

'Dave knew my personality and he could see being a sports director would be a good move for me,' White continues.

The Australian took the post in 2008, managing people who, only the year before, he'd been competing alongside. From his racing career, he had some examples to go off.

'I had some really good sports directors that I worked with, and I had some really bloody average ones,' White says. 'Some of them were glorified taxi drivers.'

Prior to his role as a DS, the Tour had been somewhat of a taunt for White.

In 2001, he was selected to compete with Armstrong's US Postal team, but then 48 hours before he was due to leave for the race the team changed its mind.

'They wanted to take one more climber instead of one more guy for the flat,' White recalls. 'My dad was already on an aeroplane from Australia to come over and watch the Tour, and they changed their mind.'

US Postal won the Tour with Armstrong and White ultimately decided he'd have to find a new team if he wanted to compete there. In 2004 he transferred to the French squad Cofidis and was again selected.

White made it to the start of Tour de France that year, which started with a prologue in Liege, Belgium where it had been raining. The morning of the Grand Depart White was warming up on a time trial bike.

'There was a cable just on the finish line and it had a metal casing over it, and it was wet, and my front wheel slipped on the metal casing,' he recalls.

'I went straight over the handlebars, knocked myself out,

broke my collarbone and woke up in a Liege hospital four hours before the start.

'I had no helmet on, nothing, so I don't remember anything.'

In hospital White had to choose to either make his Tour debut injured or go home and prepare for the Olympic Games in Athens. He didn't need surgery and his team doctor told him he could try to start the prologue that afternoon.

'But the problem is, in that edition of the Tour de France, there were cobbles on stage three or four,' White recalls.

'He said, "Look, if you do start you might get through the first couple of days but if you ride on those cobbles with that unstable fracture, it's not going to work."'

White's Tour debut was delayed in the eleventh hour again and the team had just a few hours to find a replacement for him.

'Which is actually a funny story,' he says.

'The only guy who was in distance of Liege was the oldest member of the team, he was thirty-six years old, and he was a hundred kilometres away. So, they rang him, told him to pack his bags and they got a police escort out to his house and drove him to the start.

'They had to put him as one of the last riders in the team in the prologue, so he just made it,' White continues.

'He was watching a motocross race with his family, got the phone call, "You're doing the Tour de France in three and a half hours." The guy ended up finishing the Tour de France and got another year contract out of it as well.'

White was selected by Cofidis again in 2005 and competed in what was his first and only Tour as a bike rider.

'It's always exciting. I'd been around and done other races, been to a couple of Olympics and World Championships,' says White.

'It was the last big experience in my career, and I unfortunately had to wait until I was thirty-one to get it done.'

The Tour that year passed through Germany where fans had plenty to celebrate, able to lay claim to one of the biggest teams and some of the biggest riders of the time.

'But it was, it's a big spectacle and the year I did it in 2005 was the year we went into Germany, and I don't think I've seen, beside Yorkshire in [2014], the crowds were incredible in Germany,' White continues.

'It was the T-Mobile era, Jan Ullrich, and the German fans were incredible.'

Ullrich became the first German to win the Tour in 1997 and finished runner-up four times, but in 2013 he admitted to doping, claiming he was motivated by a desire to compete on a level playing field.

You could say White's true calling at the Tour was as a sports director though because in that capacity he's returned thirteen times, first with American Jonathan Vaughters's Slipstream team, which when he joined was a start-up that could only afford second-hand buses and trucks that would break down, and then with Australian businessman Gerry Ryan's outfit, where he remains.

'It's a nice one to tick off, to say you've done,' White continues of the Tour.

'I suppose it's more so because most people in the world know the Tour de France and unless you're into cycling a lot of people don't know what the Giro is or the Vuelta is, or other big races.

'Now looking back at it, having been on the last thirteen editions, it's just another race, but we understand the importance of it that's for sure.'

White had prior coaching experience, but the path to becoming a sports director was a steep learning curve. Ultimately his prior position in the peloton, as a self-described middleman, helped to inform his style.

'I really liked that one-on-one interaction with the guys. I could understand young guys and how they were adapting to our sport,' he says.

'I was mates with Lance Armstrong and some of the biggest athletes in our sport, and some of those big champions, they struggled to understand people who struggled, or they struggled to understand why people can't deliver like they do because they haven't got the talent.

'That's why I think you don't see a lot of big stars in our sport become sports directors,' White continues. 'They have a very different outlook on what is possible because they're only looking at themselves and what it takes for them to be champions, or for them to achieve things at a high level.

'They don't often have a good grasp of the other people.'

In the team car, White will speak to the director next to him, listen to Piquet's updates, and take calls from scouts who may be at different points on the route, relaying information back on the roads, or the weather. He'll look at maps, data, and talk to his riders, always weighing up strategies, moves and countermoves while driving hundreds of kilometres a day.

It's a role that has developed and progressed along with the sport.

'Sports directors of the nineties,' White says, 'they were

doing everything – they were the ones booking the flights, some of them were coaching, they were doing tactics, logistics.

'In the 2000s the teams didn't just have two sports directors who did every race on the calendar, they had four directors, or they had media people, or started bringing in coaches, or sports scientists.'

Now the role is different again.

'The big difference is the amount of support staff that you have compared to thirteen years ago, and you're managing a lot more people now,' he says.

'It's managing people and it's also managing your athletes. Tactics is a very important part of it. In our team now I think ninety-five per cent of our riders are coached internally, so you're having less day-to-day contact with the athletes than thirteen years ago.

'Back then I was coaching Cam Meyer, I was coaching Chris Sutton, athletes. I enjoyed it but no sports director I don't think is now a coach.'

White is friends with renowned coaches and managers, like rugby union identity Eddie Jones, and has looked to other sports for inspiration.

'I think Eddie has been with us at a couple of Tours, and Trent Robinson [NRL premiership-winning coach] has been at races with me, and they say they always take something away from a different sport,' White says.

'With the way we operate, it's very niche. There is no other sport like cycling as far as our logistics and travel and the way we are a mobile circus.

'It's like, for those guys, the best way for me to describe the Tour de France is it's like playing a grand final twenty-one days in a row. And they struggle to get their heads around that, those coaches, because the most they play is once a week in those sorts of sports. If there is something special, it might be two.

'But they just are amazed at how we do our thing,' White continues. 'Pack up, move on to the next hotel, have our meeting, do our race, the communication we have in the car, we debrief trying to get as much information as we can, and then press reset and do it again three weeks in a row.'

White has learned things from coaches belonging to other codes over the years, but his biggest takeaway has been in people management.

'That's a big part of my role,' he says.

'I've got so many specialist people I work with, in coaching, sports science, nutrition, that they're the ones giving that information, not me anymore. It's about managing that group.'

I think back to the team car I passed when I was sitting on the back of the motorbike, cruising through the convoy, and how the preoccupied directors inside were oblivious to me peering in.

I had this assumption once that there was as much wheeling and dealing between sports directors in the convoy as there were riders on the road. At one point I believed that the directors, more than anyone else in the race, controlled what happened.

At the Tour Down Under, years before I had covered a stage at the Tour de France, I was sitting in the passenger seat of Highroad's team car, which former rider and sports director Allan Peiper was driving. Another car drove up alongside us and Peiper wound down his window to speak to his rival counterpart at the steering wheel.

The pair spoke in Flemish and I assumed they were talking tactics and didn't want me to understand. It was a jovial exchange so for all I know they actually could have just been saying, 'Hi, how was your winter? Yeah, I drew the short straw with the journo riding shotgun today.'

But that day at the Tour years later, manoeuvring through the convoy, there were no open windows, no chat between the rival sports directors.

Chat, cooperation, or collusion, as White refers to it, between teams is part of a bygone era.

Fifteen years ago, White says, the peloton was largely constructed from teams belonging to traditional cycling nations – Italy, France, Belgium, the Netherlands. It was common then for Italian teams to work together, for French teams to work together and so on.

'There were a lot more links from team to team,' says White.

'I think now with our sport being live nearly start to finish, with the amount of money in our sport, I think there's a lot less talk between teams.'

There are exceptions.

'Obviously if you're in a sprint team and you've got a sprinter and its Lotto, Quick-Step and someone else, of course they're going to help each other out, and as soon as the break goes, they're going to put someone on the front – that's normal,' he says.

'They've got the same idea, they want to make sure it's a sprint, they want to support their sprinter and so it's no use fighting it. If you've got one of the world's best sprinters, you're going to help chase.'

Teams are inclined to work together when they have the same goal and the same tactic to reach it during a stage but that's where it seems to start and end.

'I think gone are those days where teams really help other teams unless it is in that they have the same goal,' says White.

'Why? Because at the end of the day, how do you work with another team and then go back to your sponsors, or if someone asks you, "What are you doing today?" "Oh, well, we have to help this team because they helped us last week."

'Sponsors don't understand that. The media maybe doesn't understand that.'

The increased media coverage of the Tour and introduction of live broadcasts of stages from beginning to end has influenced how the convoy operates, even though the procession of cars itself is never in focus on screen.

'Before television was highlight packages, or the last two hours of the race, there was a lot more collusion, there were more blocks of teams in blocks of countries where that was happening, but I think these days it happens very, very rarely,' White says.

Peiper also says that the race he knew in the 1980s is different to the one riders contest now. The Tour has become even more commercial and the professionalism of the teams has evolved with that. As such, the competition is tighter, and the leeway riders allow each other smaller.

'A rider could never ride away alone and take twenty minutes and put on the yellow jersey. It's never going to happen these days because it's so important,' Peiper says.

'Years ago, it was so laid back. It was more or less fun being a bike rider, but I don't know how much fun it is now.'

Although White notes that there are some things about the Tour that have not changed.

'The prize money is the same – fifteen years later. And I'm not joking. It hasn't changed since 1999,' he laughs.

But overall the sport has evolved into a richer, more global industry composed of people from every continent, save for Antarctica. It has also become more individualised, which, above all else, is what directors manage.

'It's such a dynamic group, that you're on the road for so long as well, and it does boil down to having the right personalities and the right people in those roles,' White says.

'I think it goes back to how does the team function as well. And it is brought back to recruitment, if you're recruiting the right people – riders and staff.

'You look at teams, you hear people from other teams, and some teams they're not the nicest place to work, it's not a real positive environment, and we're all under pressure.'

That attitude is reflected in the riders that White manages as well, and was something Michael Matthews, when talking about mentors upon his return to BikeExchange in 2021, mentioned.

'Having Whitey in the team, his passion for the Tour is definitely something special,' says Matthews.

'You can bounce ideas off him, whether it's good or bad he'll give you an honest opinion back. But a lot of the *soigneurs* and mechanics also are amazing people who you can talk to. Whether it's a super high positive, or a really low negative, they'll help you with it. I love that about this team. Everyone is equal; no one is above each other.'

Cycling is not like football, or soccer, where the sports

directors get the axe if a team doesn't perform at the Tour. There are plenty of teams that don't perform. Of the twenty-three squads that competed at the 2021 edition, only eight recorded victories.

'The pressure on results, it boils back to management, for sure, but at the end of the day the guys who are getting the job done are the riders, they're the guys crossing the finish line first, and everyone around them – we're just here to support them,' says White.

However, there is still an expectation on directors and results arguably mean more in cycling because of its dependence on sponsorship.

'Teams are judged pretty harshly on what they do in the Tour. And a lot of people can forget the other nine months of the season if you have one good result at the Tour. Good or bad,' White adds.

In some instances the longevity of teams comes down to the whims of the rich businesspeople who own them. When Russian billionaire Oleg Tinkov entered the sport, he described the team he took over from Bjarne Riis as his 'toy'. He reduced the livelihood of hard-working men and women to an inanimate, expendable object. Tinkov eventually gleaned enough marketing exposure for his Tinkoff Bank, which was naming sponsor, and grew frustrated with how the sport was governed.

He withdrew his sponsorship at the end of the 2016 season, and the team folded. The next time I heard anything about him was in 2021 when he was convicted of tax fraud in the US and forced to pay a penalty of US$508,936,184 (more than $700 million Australian).

But when White talks of his day-to-day routine and performance outcomes he refers again to people management rather than tactical playbooks or the fancies of benefactors.

'If you're making the wrong decisions, wrong selections, wrong roster picks, it falls back onto management one hundred per cent,' White continues.

'You've got to make on-the-spot calls, some are right, some are wrong. You've got a certain amount of information at your fingertips, and you've got to make those calls.

'If you're not confident in making those calls, you're probably in the wrong seat in the car,' he continues.

'You've got to trust people. Trust people to do the work, do their job and, even in the most high-pressure environment, you can still enjoy what you're doing.'

CHAPTER 10
THE ULTIMATE SACRIFICE

Belgian racer Jens Debusschere had been told that his French teammate Bryan Coquard was done.

The pair were newly acquainted. Debusschere had joined Coquard's B&B Hotels–Vital Concept team in 2020 following a single season at Katusha and a long tenure supporting André Greipel at Lotto–Soudal.

Those years racing with Greipel comprise the fondest memories of his career. He describes how the relationships between teammates slowly and steadily built over time, from acquaintances to teammates and then friends who shared a special bond, always on the road together.

By comparison, Debusschere had been competing with Coquard for about six months when the pair joined forces at the 2020 Tour.

It was stage 17 from Grenoble to the Col de la Loze mountain pass near the enchanting Méribel ski resort in the Alps.

The sprinters were not the story that day, especially with

what was happening at the front of the race. Colombian Miguel Ángel López won the stage ahead of Primož Roglič and Tadej Pogačar. Three days later, Pogačar would steal the yellow jersey from Roglič on the penultimate stage, to win his career first Tour title ahead of his Slovenian counterpart, and Australian veteran Richie Porte.

The route to the summit finish was nasty. The Col de la Loze topped out at 2304 metres and was the highest peak of that Tour. It came after the Col de la Madeleine, which was also classified as a *hors catégorie* climb. Mountains at the Tour are graded, or categorised, in terms of difficulty. A *hors catégorie* translates to 'beyond categorisation'. It is the toughest climb there is, the 'if you look up, you'll meet your maker face to face' kind of deal.

Debusschere's job that day was to get into the *grupetto* with Coquard and make it to the finish line within the time limit.

Staying in the *grupetto* does not guarantee you safe passage to tomorrow but it's your best shot.

Behind that group is wilderness.

Debusschere was in the *grupetto*, comfortable with the pace that was being set, when he realised Coquard wasn't there. He'd clocked Coquard's rival Sam Bennett, who had four or five teammates banded around to ensure the Irishman would get through the difficult stage as effortlessly as possible, but not his man.

Debusschere considered Coquard to be a better climber than himself and so assumed he was fine and further up the road.

'Then suddenly I heard he was already two or three minutes behind our *grupetto*, and we were only at the start of the first climb of the day, so I knew it was going to be hard, but I waited anyway,' says Debusschere.

With the imposing Col de la Madeleine ahead, Debusschere, unfathomably, dropped back several minutes to Coquard.

As Debusschere slowed and the *grupetto* pedalled further and further away towards the shadow of the Col de Madeleine, one of his former Lotto–Soudal sports directors drove up alongside him in a team car, with an observation on Coquard.

'He told me, "Don't wait for him because he's not going to make it. I saw him already; he's really struggling and he's not going to make it,"' Debusschere recalls.

He waited anyway and dropped back even further until he saw Coquard, who was labouring alone, doubting his own ability to continue.

'He told me twice, or three times, to go back to the *grupetto*. But I told him no. "If you're out of time cut, then me also. We're just going to finish with two, even if it's ten minutes out of time cut."'

Debusschere is at his home in Belgium when he recalls the experience over the phone more than a year later. Very few times have I been speechless in an interview before but the more he talks, the more my mouth drops in disbelief.

The obvious question is why. Why do this? Coquard, by his own admission and the observation of others, was done. And it's not like at this point the duo were best buds. Sure, Debusschere makes a living from helping Coquard to win races, and races within races, but there has to be a point you draw a line. If it was for his Lotto blood brothers, or if Debusschere had his own inkling that he wasn't going to survive the day, then I'd get it. But that wasn't the case. So why?

I don't normally talk up athletes, nor have I ever bought into the notion of illustrating them as immortals, or gladiators, titans or gods. They've always been regular people to me. There are mountain stages in the Tour though that are so ridiculous I shake my head at what riders do.

Debusschere gets where I'm going and recalls his Tour campaign with Katusha the year before, in 2019, when the team, without Marcel Kittel, was at a loss and told him to have a crack at the sprints instead, with Russian climber Ilnur Zakarin focused on a top-ten result on general classification (he finished fifty-first).

'I did a Tour de France on my own without a sprinter by my side and that didn't work, so why would I continue without a sprinter in this Tour?' Debusschere says.

He is one of those riders who has done the Tour enough to not be in awe of it. His relationship with it is somewhere between love and hate, like many seasoned campaigners. However, a start in the race is still not something he takes for granted.

Having set the tone with Coquard, Debusschere got on with his job, trying everything to get himself and Coquard back to the *grupetto* after they cleared the Madeleine, manoeuvred through the descent, and hit a long valley. Debusschere, with Coquard on his wheel, set the pace all the way to the Col de la Loze. In that time Coquard was able to recover somewhat, but by the foot of the climb Debusschere was dead.

'During the valley we didn't speak so much because I was also on the limit. We started the last climb, and I was still pulling. He told me we can go faster otherwise we don't make it and then I said, "At the moment I cannot go faster, this is my pace for the whole climb, so if you want to be in time, if you think you can make it, you should go,"' Debusschere recalls.

'And then they went, him and the [team] car. I told the car stay with him, give me two bottles and I will make it, I will give it my all to the top. But it wasn't enough.

'I could hold this pace to the top, but I couldn't accelerate anymore. The legs were just empty.

'At the end, he was just in, and I fell out of time cut.'

The Tour is one of two races on the calendar, including Paris–Roubaix, that riders will insist on finishing rather than admitting defeat and climbing off their bicycles. Debusschere didn't give up after Coquard rode away to finish dead last within the time limit, thirty-five minutes and forty-five seconds behind the stage winner Lopez.

On the Col de la Loze, Debusschere was crunching numbers, looking at his power meter to check his power output, taking in his condition, and calculating if he could, even though he felt empty, make it. He still had his earpiece in and updates on where those ahead of him stood came over the race radio.

'They gave the time through the radios like, "You're at four kilometres to the top and you still have fifteen minutes, or no worries," and then I was thinking, "Yeah, I'm still seven kilometres from the top, so it will be hard. I need to accelerate now,"' Debusschere says.

'I tried for one kilometre to get the watts up, but it didn't work. It was quite a struggle in my mind also, especially only looking at the watts and trying to get in at time.'

Debusschere accepted with 1000 metres of the 170-kilometre slugfest remaining that his Tour de France was over.

'A climb that steep is for sure four to five minutes per kilometre, so I knew I was going to be around four minutes late, but, anyway, this was only one kilometre [to go], so I continued.'

Debusschere crossed the finish line ahead of the broom wagon. The broom wagon, *voiture balais* in French or sag wagon as it is also known in English, is a vehicle that travels at the very back of each stage. Like death, it lurks, ready to sweep up those who fall out of the *grupetto* or out of the convoy and face the fate of finishing the stage and abandoning the race or abandoning on the route and climbing into death's fold.

But Debusschere was not completely broken.

He has only been reduced to tears once at the Tour, in 2019, when he and then Katusha teammate Alex Dowsett were quick to be dropped and only made the time cut because the mountain stage to Tignes that day was shortened due to a landslide en route to the original finish. It's his worst memory of the race.

'We were alone, ten minutes back on the *grupetto*, and we were lost until they told us, "You have to give it your all to the top of this climb and they take the time on this climb, and you don't need to do the last one." Then, we still had a chance, so we went full up, but we were broken.

'On the top of that climb was the first time and the only time I really cried after a stage, or after a bike race. I don't know if it was because I was lucky, or if it was because I was angry. It was one of the two.'

But on the Col de la Loze, on terrain most people traverse high above in a cable car, Debusschere wasn't sprinting to make it, as he already knew he was going to be late.

Once he reached the summit, thirty-seven minutes and thirty-five seconds behind Lopez, and one minute and nineteen seconds behind Coquard, he'd already recovered a little bit.

The Tour demands sacrifice but there is usually a dividend to be made from that investment. In Debusschere's case on the Col de la Loze that wasn't so. His was the ultimate sacrifice; he is sure that, had he not waited for Coquard, he would have finished stage 17 within the time cut. He would not have been the very last man to cross the line. He would not have been packing his bags and going home.

'The thing is, I learned we always do it like this; if the sprinter is in trouble you wait for him and that's the thing to do,' Debusschere says.

'The team didn't tell me how far he was back; didn't tell me I should wait. It was fully my decision and that's, in my opinion, the only right way to be a lead-out man or a helper. So, there was no choice, or nothing else going on in my head: just wait for him and try to get him in.'

Once he'd done his job, Debusschere could have pulled over to the side of the road, climbed off his bike on the Col de la Loze and stopped suffering, but he didn't. Even in that lonely limbo, knowing that his fate was sealed, he kept going.

It was the same for Nic Dlamini, the first black South African to compete at the Tour, during the 2021 edition. On the first day in the Alps where Australian Ben O'Connor prevailed, Dlamini, pelted by rain, riding through low cloud, in conditions that had turned dark and wintry, refused to stop. The headlights of his Qhubeka NextHash team car following behind lit the road ahead. Dlamini crossed the finish line about ninety minutes down on O'Connor and more than forty minutes behind the time cut at the finish in Tignes, where organisers were apparently already taking down gantry.

Riders say they persevere in honour of, or respect for, the Tour, even though it really only loves back the one per cent. Their pain isn't recorded either. The results sheet doesn't show that Dlamini laboured for more than an hour to cross the line; it doesn't recognise Debusschere's selfless plight. The results sheet just reads that they finished out of the time limit – 'OOT'.

For sprinter Robbie McEwen, the prospect of stopping mid-stage always served as negative reinforcement that helped him to outlast the torture and survive the mountains. At the Tour and during Paris–Roubaix, he insisted, where physically and mentally possible, on finishing, just to finish.

'The hardest thing I did at the Tour, other than completing some really, really tough mountain stages was completing the '04 Tour with two fractures in my back,' McEwen recalls.

'I always went back to images that I saw when I first started watching the Tour, of guys having their [race] number peeled off and in the back of the sag wagon, and also the way that I thought of guys who had pulled out.

'I just thought to myself, "Yes, it's hard; yes, it's excruciating; yes, psychologically, it's a terrible place to be. But if you're not sick or injured and you just pull out, you're weak as piss." That kept me going. I didn't want people to think I was just weak as piss.'

Smashing yourself like that can have longer-term conse-quences though. We know more about these now, and riders are savvier to them.

Battered, bruised and red raw from road rash, Roglič

abandoned the 2021 Tour to heal and focus on the upcoming men's time trial at the Tokyo Olympics and the Vuelta a España, both of which he won.

However, the notion of finishing or trying to finish the Tour, even if it defies logic, is still prevalent.

I've seen riders literally wincing in pain behind the start line as they take off every day. American Taylor Phinney arrived one year on the Champs-Élysées with an eye so black, so swollen, that there is a photo of me standing in a huddle of journalists around him, cringing at how sore it looked.

'You learn some really important lessons about perseverance, and it hardens you, even if it's embarrassing to finish,' McEwen says.

Making sacrifices for others is arguably easier when you know you're good enough to help the best sprinter, the best climber, but just not quite good enough to be that person yourself. As Michael Mørkøv and Debusschere say, when your leader is winning and you've played a part in that, your investment is rewarded. It's worth it.

The sacrifices where riders give up their own chances for larger team objectives, even though they know they could win a stage themselves, is a greater ask.

There was only one time Mathew Hayman felt like that, in the final Tour of his career in 2018.

Stage 9 that year went through northern France and finished in Roubaix, where two years earlier he'd won the 'Hell of the North'. It featured cobblestone sectors that Hayman through his deep affinity and affliction with the spring classic and Monument, one of the longest, oldest, most prestigious one-day races on the calendar, inherently knew.

If there was ever a chance for him to win a stage of the Tour de France, it was arguably this moment.

But despite his knowledge, passion, and aptitude, he had been tasked with supporting title contender Adam Yates, who the tricky terrain presented a danger to.

'[That] was probably the only time that I felt I could have had the legs to really do something. But we were riding GC, so I had to stay with Yatesy,' Hayman recalls.

'I accepted it there. And you know that, going in, you know that's one of the reasons you've been selected for the race, and I value that in other people, so I need to do it.'

Hayman was in the twilight of his career at the 2018 Tour; he retired the next season and didn't have the worry of securing a contract. Proving himself before the trade window officially opened in August wasn't necessary. Yet he was still a competitor, he knew what winning felt like, what supporting others to victory felt like, and the difference.

'[It's] only really that one day, in the whole Tours de France I've ridden, in Roubaix, where I've really felt it would have been nice to have been let off the chain,' Hayman says.

'In that situation I was giving up my opportunities and I was clearly better than the person at that particular stage. I knew when they were going to go, I knew which guys, and I wasn't the only one,' Hayman continues.

'There were four or five of us that were sitting there with our hands tied and we were watching other guys ride away there. You knew where it was going to happen.'

The cobbles were familiar to Hayman, he competed over them every season at the classics.

But they weren't familiar to general classification riders, who needed assistance to get through unscathed, and that is where Hayman found his return on his investment that day.

'In the same breath, hats off to all the GC guys that got through that stage,' Hayman continues.

'I was very surprised at how well they did. Yes, they're fully supported by guys that know those roads and know how to race the classics, but they put themselves out there and were all there in the final.'

The 2015 Paris–Roubaix winner John Degenkolb won stage 9 that year. Yates came in safely in twenty-seventh and finished the Tour overall in twenty-ninth place on general classification.

Debusschere opted not to return to the Tour de France in 2021. The idea of suffering for three weeks straight became less justifiable.

I often think you must have an addictive personality to work at the Tour. It becomes not just a job, but a lifestyle sustained by hits of high stakes emotion and adrenaline. That all started to have less of an effect on Debusschere.

'If you don't really have a great job to do at the Tour then why actually even bother to go?' he asks rhetorically.

'I mean, if you're not a super sprinter or a super climber or something in-between, you can win stages in the middle mountains, then actually, yeah, if you don't have a specific role in the team and in the Tour then I guess it's better to not go.

'I didn't want to be … one guy just sitting in the bunch, getting to Paris and being destroyed afterwards for just being there. Of course, it's nice to finish another Tour but you need to have a purpose to do it also.'

Debusschere admits that, in the lead-up to the 2021 Grand Depart, he started to fear he was going to miss out, started to question whether he did want to compete at the race.

In the end he wasn't selected and, as he watched the rain-soaked, crash-heavy edition from his home while preparing for end of season races, he felt relieved.

Would he ever go back, I wondered to myself, in a team still successful but less prolific than the giddy days of Greipel winning surplus stages?

That in essence is what Debusschere was sacrificing himself for: wins, but also mateship. The lifestyle.

When I asked how he pulled himself together after crying at the finish in Tignes that day with Dowsett, Debusschere emphasises the importance of having good teammates and a positive surrounding.

'All the guys made me laugh the first minute we got back,' he recalls.

'Cyclists also forget a lot, and fast. That's why we are all wanting to go to the Tour, except for the week after the Tour.

'I forgot about it the day after, and then the day after was also a shortened [stage], and then everybody was like, "Come on, you have to make it, it's only one more push and then you are there." Mentally it's not so hard anymore to survive that one. The worst has passed.'

CHAPTER 11
THE WARHORSE WHO WON

Cadel Evans committed years of his life to winning the yellow jersey and his battle to become Australia's first Tour de France champion meant he was always a source of interest and an object of attention. There were times at the Tour when he felt like he was treated as less than an animal and he resorted to drastic measures to switch off after stages.

'In the most extreme situations, [I'd] sit in the bathroom with headphones on and lock the door. But that's getting pretty bad when you have to do that,' he says.

'My good Tours, and when I was with BMC, I would read a book in the evening, but nothing to do with cycling. I'd read a non-fiction history [book].'

One of those was about Captain Cook's voyage to Australia.

'It's a whole world away, which is really what I need,' he continues.

'If I was rooming by myself [I'd] listen to some music, and if I was rooming with someone else [I'd] lie on the bed and read a book just to get your mind completely away because you turn on the TV and it's talking about the Tour, you call home in Australia, they're talking about the Tour.'

The retired all-rounder copped it more than most.

Evans's Tour debut was in 2005 when he finished eighth behind Lance Armstrong. In 2006 he finished fourth on general classification, then he was runner-up in 2007 and second to Carlos Sastre in 2008. In 2009, when he didn't want to be at the race and relations with his then-team Silence–Lotto were at best frayed, he came twenty-ninth. On debut with BMC in 2010 he placed twenty-fifth, which may have worked out differently if he hadn't broken his arm after stopping on the roadside for a leak. Finally, he made history with his victory in 2011.

Evans was watching the first week of the 2021 Tour from his home in Europe when he recalled with photographic-like memory key moments from each of his Tours.

Even though he came second, he says, '2008 was my hardest Tour ever. I had a crash early on and was holding not bad injuries, but they slowed me down.

'In some ways it was my best ride at the Tour because, for the ability I had, I got a good result. But everyone was disappointed around me because I didn't win, and they were expecting me, or wanting me, to win.'

That Tour was effectively decided when Sastre pulled away on Alpe d'Huez, won the queen stage (the stage which is deemed the hardest of the race) and assumed the yellow jersey from his CSC–Saxo Bank teammate Frank Schleck.

'The stage to Alpe d'Huez, trying to close the gap to Carlos Sastre, that was the hardest hour I've ever had on my bike in my life,' Evans continues.

He swiftly moves on.

'[In] 2009 I had a lot of troubles in the lead-in with my team. It was a Tour I didn't even want to be at. I was in an environment that wasn't friendly, and I was getting the blame for everything that was going wrong and that wasn't nice.'

Evans's team environment changed in 2010 with his move to BMC and it was reflected in his results.

At BMC, American George Hincapie became his main guy in the race. Hincapie was a former chief lieutenant to Armstrong and was a commanding figure who could part the peloton like Moses parted water. Evans had complete confidence in him, sure he would help him get through tricky stages.

'He just looked out for me,' Evans says.

'And then, behind the scenes, I had the faith of the management and *director sportif*. There was never a discussion; if I felt we should do something tactically or strategically, it was like, "Okay, we'll do that."'

Evans believes he was close that season.

'But break your arm then ride into the yellow jersey and try and defend the yellow jersey in the Alps, with a broken arm, it's not realistic, not ideal,' he continues.

'That was a luck thing. I stopped for a biological break, and I was trying to move through the peloton, and someone cut through the inside and took me out. I wasn't even in the peloton; I was behind it coming back through the convoy.' Evans had injured himself on stage 8 before the first rest day, and on stage 9 hid his condition from the media, no one apparently questioning why he had blue kinesio tape secured all up his forearm until he dropped out of title contention and arrived at the finish distressed.

In Australia, Evans was tantamount to the Tour, and abroad he was, for a long stint, the leader of teams belonging to one of cycling's traditional heartlands, Belgium, where supporters are fanatical about the sport. It's their football, AFL, NRL.

Some cyclists thrive off that attention; I'd go so far as to say Armstrong's biggest fear is being obsolete. Evans, on the other hand, did not totally enjoy it, and while he had the physical talent and mental fortitude of the best there were many factors that worked against him before his eventual success.

He competed at a time when cycling was on the precipice of evolution and change but doping, we now know, was still prevalent and put Evans at a disadvantage.

He laughs when I ask why some people of his era took that path when sports science was, granted, not as widespread and commonly used as it is today, but still available. Armstrong did ride with a power meter in 1999 to 2000, I'm told.

'You could go faster with higher-octane fuel,' Evans says.

'In physiology we knew that as well because we can measure that. But it was also a real mentality thing within the sport.'

He doesn't begrudge those rivals who apparently paid more attention to their hematocrit levels – the portion of red cells in your blood – than what they ate, how they trained, or what technology they used.

'I don't think it makes me as angry as much as people think,' Evans says.

'I probably have more anger or even hurt for the criticism I received for not being able to follow some particular riders, or not being able to race as convincingly as other riders did.

'I had this thing for years, "The rider who never attacks,"' he continues.

'I'm just like, if I'm going flat out just to stay in the wheels in eighth or [with] someone on a hilltop finish, what hope have I even got of attacking them? But I was criticised and insulted for that.'

Evans knows the criticism wasn't personal; it reflected the mentality in and around the sport at the time.

'When you have a mentality like that, obviously, instead of looking at your watts per kilogram you're looking at your hematocrit and judging by what you can or can't do, you're also psyching yourself out as well, or undermining your own confidence is a better way to say it,' he says.

However, it still shaped his Tour campaigns.

'I probably had more anger about that than other things. I can't change the whole world singlehandedly!'

Evans was thirty-four when he won the yellow jersey and stood on the podium drenched in golden summer sunlight as famous Australian singer Tina Arena serenaded him in a reception no winner has since received.

One of Arena's greatest hits is the ballad 'Chains', and that day all of Evans's shackles finally came off.

'She contacted the Tour organisation and asked if she could sing the national anthem and they agreed to it,' Evans recalls.

It's one of few things he does remember in the aftermath of his win.

'For me, from the moment I crossed the finish line of that Tour de France, the next few weeks of my life were a complete blur because it was a bit out of control.

'I was standing on the podium, and she looked up and smiled, "Hey, you were awesome buddy, great job." And then she started singing the national anthem.

'When there's a hundred thousand people standing around you it's a unique lifetime experience, put it that way.'

Evans had won a stage at Mur-de-Bretagne earlier in the campaign and then ridden into the *maillot jaune* on the penultimate stage time trial.

'Riding onto the Champs-Élysées, crossing the line with George and all the guys in 2011, those moments were just incredible,' he says.

'The Mur-de-Bretagne stage, getting taken down the side of the group, passing the entire peloton on [Marcus] Burghardt's wheel to come to the front, get led-out by George at the bottom of the climb and win the stage, moments like that I'll probably never forget.'

On the tenth anniversary of his victory, Evans remained the third-oldest winner of the Tour, since its first running in 1903, behind 1922 champion Firmin Lambot, who was thirty-six when he claimed the yellow jersey, and Henri Pelissier, the Frenchman who triumphed the following season also at thirty-four.

It was Belgian Lambot's second victory after he won his maiden title in 1919, when the Tour resumed following a four-year hiatus due to World War I. I can't imagine what riding through war-ravaged France would have looked like, you can still feel the ghosts of lost soldiers in some parts today, but pictures depict competitors, like Lambot and Pelissier, competing with cigarettes hanging from their mouths and tyre tubes wrapped around their shoulders.

It's far removed from the technology and sports nutrition that was at Evans's disposal and which he adopted, despite being mocked for it then.

'Crossing the finish line and pressing my set button on my SRM [power metre] when I was racing, other competitors would laugh at you,' he says.

'I didn't put sugar in my tea, I would use fructose or honey. Instead of having pasta every day I would alternate with having rice as different carbohydrates, the whole gluten thing. And people would laugh at you. Now, absolutely everyone on every team does that, so it's changed.'

Evans firmly believes that, until 2010, his biggest weakness was that he didn't have a strong team. But he had a multitude of strengths.

'I was really, really hungry as an athlete. I wanted it, really, really badly. I say that now, years later, looking back at myself as a self-analysis,' he says.

'I had a certain amount of physical ability to time trial and climb, and a lot of varied racing experience.

'My biggest strength was my consistency but some of my teammates would say my biggest strength was I could hurt more than anyone else. In the words of Chris Horner, he said, "You're good and all but you hurt yourself more than anyone else out there."'

Evans was also able to adapt to whatever role the Tour demanded of him.

'I'd like to think I was a reasonably rounded package where I could do one-day races, three-week races, race in the cold, race in the heat, race in the snow. I could climb, but I could still get through the messy stuff on the flats,' he says.

'I completely changed my mentality to adapt to the situation needed at the time. The day of a time trial my mentality was, "Okay, today I'm a time trialist." A mountain stage, "Okay, today I'm a climber." The downhill finish, "Okay, today I'm a downhill mountain biker again,"' he says, referencing his first foray into cycling. 'On a flat day, these days in Bretagne, "Okay, today I'm going to be a classics rider."'

However, cycling is fundamentally a team sport and, as we've seen, the power and dedication of the people behind you is crucial.

'Many of my campaigns, and I think it's fair to say, when there's fifty guys less in the mountains and I'm the only guy on GC who doesn't have a teammate, it's fair to say maybe you weren't so well supported,' Evans says.

That was a common observation when Evans was competing but talking to him a decade after his victory, and six years after his retirement in 2015, it seems to me that dealing with aspects of the Tour that were outside of his control, the kind he'd try to escape from in the bathroom, were bigger challenges than the multifaceted fights he faced in the race on the road.

There is more than one video of Evans on YouTube sharply reacting to random people who, prior to the COVID-19 pandemic, stood at such a proximity that they could, and would, reach out and physically touch him.

'When you're a Tour favourite, to get to the start line, this is pre-COVID of course, people would be grabbing your jersey and they're pulling you left and right. If you don't stop for them, they get angry at you and they abuse you,' he says.

Evans was somewhat vulnerable to words, being called things like 'the rider who never attacks', but he particularly resented his personal space being encroached upon. He speaks about it now from a viewpoint of compassion, but still can't reconcile with the intrusion of his space.

'It was more just the physical aspect of people wanting your time and attention, and not respecting that you're riding the Tour de France and you deserve to have eight hours of sleep, some rest and some time to yourself,' he says.

'Having to lock yourself in the room and not answer anyone who knocks on the door or anything, just to get some time away from it all, was what for me was stressful.'

Evans, I imagine, would have loved, if not prospered from, competing for the yellow jersey during the pandemic when restrictions that distanced the riders from everyone else to protect their health were enforced.

'You're going to work like anyone else going to work at the end of the day. On a human level that gets completely forgotten about and that's what, for me, I found draining,' he says.

* * *

Evans is pushing a different set of wheels when we speak over the phone during the tenth anniversary of his Tour win.

I was on my way to the start of stage 4 of the 2021 Tour, and he was out on a walk in Switzerland, where he lives, with two of his kids sitting in a black double pram.

There was a time in the lead-up to his retirement where Evans couldn't even say the 'R' word let alone speak about life after cycling, which he's since found sweet.

He sporadically says hello in Italian to people as he passes them out on the walk and later emails me a picture of the pram. It's a symbol of how his life has changed and how proud he is of it.

Evans is in the process of planning a reunion with the men

who helped deliver him to the yellow jersey, and their families, in Tuscany, Italy. It sounds far more sophisticated than the warm beer and late-night pizzas Hincapie came back to the team hotel with when Evans won the Tour.

Evans answers every planned and sporadic question I ask. Every time I've interviewed him in a calm setting, one-on-one with a blue-lined reporter notepad in hand, the conversation has been open and flowing.

The 2021 Tour also featured the Mur-de-Bretagne, so evoked more than one memory for him.

Evans is surprised by but grateful for the attention he's received.

'When I was stopping racing, I thought you go away and get forgotten about when you leave the sport, but I feel anything but forgotten about,' he says.

'The replays and the finish of the stage to Mur-de-Bretagne, I'm sitting there watching Eurosport coverage of the Tour de France and I see myself on the TV, it's kind of bizarre but it's been nice to be remembered and nice to look back as well.'

Evans, like many others who have suffered the pain to enjoy the privilege of competing in and working at the Tour, had a love–hate relationship with the race.

'If things didn't come together in 2011 it probably would have been more hate than love but, fortunately, having the success there and the experience and a great group of guys to go for the win with, and share the victory with, that really made it,' he says.

'It erased a lot of hate memories, moments of stress and absurd expectations and being treated like absolute,' he pauses, 'not even like being treated like an animal.

'And the fact that we're still talking about it now ten years later.'

Evans's greatest fear was regret, and he was driven by it. It ultimately became his underlying motivation, why he never gave up on winning the *maillot jaune*.

'I always looked to be a professional cyclist, a professional athlete, as an opportunity – an opportunity to do my best and give my all,' he explains.

'I never wanted to have regrets.

'Earlier in my career, one of the first good professionals I met and got to know seemed to have a real chip on his shoulder towards the sport. Here I was hoping to become a professional and follow in his footsteps and I thought, "I never want to have anger or disdain towards the sport that I love."'

Evans had days where he was disappointed, had bad luck or lost.

'Maybe I got beaten by people who weren't behaving, who weren't respecting all the rules or something, but at the same time I had this opportunity to race my bike for a living and make a career out of it,' he says.

'It was way better than paying my own way to go to small races in Australia and not have time to train properly.

'In that regard, I always looked at it as a great opportunity I was really fortunate to have, make the most of it and then, most of all, not have any regrets afterwards.'

Evans's early Tour title attempts were before my time as a cycling journalist, but he had a home on the coast in Barwon Heads, which he travelled back to most pre-seasons, near Geelong where I moved to do my cadetship.

So, he became a regular focus for me, and the local paper,

which was serendipitous given in 2011 Evans had the season of his life winning the Tour as well as the World Championships.

I interviewed him after those wins on live national television from Federation Square in Melbourne where thousands of people had turned out to his homecoming, even though cycling isn't a mainstream sport in Australia and, outside of the Tour and the Tour Down Under, doesn't get a lot of commercial press.

My lasting memory of Evans though is an interview I did with him at the 2010 Tour Down Under before his major victories in 2011.

He was sitting in the passenger seat of a team car, recovering after a stage, and I was standing outside the door waiting for the right moment to interrupt.

It was my first big road assignment, and I was in perfect position until a senior journalist from national newspaper *The Australian* blindsided me from the left and jumped in front to ask Evans questions.

He was an old-school journo and had a Fleet Street air about him, with a bushy brown moustache and deep raspy voice owing to a time smoking was allowed in newsrooms. Basically, I wasn't going to be muscling my way back in and instead stood there like a deer in headlights, berating myself afterwards for underestimating how competitive the gig was and missing the opportunity.

I asked Evans if I could add a couple more questions once my rival was done. He said something along the lines of 'Maybe later but I am tired and need to rest' before taking off. His body language said as much and so I didn't follow up.

The next morning, I received a text message from BMC team press officer Georges Luechinger asking if I wanted to have a coffee with Evans before the stage start and ask my questions.

Luechinger was exclusively appointed to manage Evans's media requests and became a great help to him.

'He'd look out for my health and wellbeing just on a human level, which seems absurd that you would even have to look for that,' Evans says. 'As an athlete, sometimes that gets completely forgotten about because it's all about your performance and presentation.'

I'd had an extra-large latte before our catch-up so the espresso Evans handed me went down like lead, but the interview was far better and more valuable than anything I would have got pushing my own agenda the day before.

I wondered if I'd pursued the interview the day before, when Evans had said he was tired, I wouldn't have got it the next day.

It's hard to marry the image of Evans beaming on the podium in the yellow jersey or fighting against some of the world's best cyclists on all terrain and in all conditions with the image of a man pushed into hiding in a confined space for a moment of peace.

But that happened when his routines around racing were interrupted and he employed measures to protect precious down time, which he obviously viewed as integral to his performance, and maybe even sanity.

'I've always looked at it quite methodically: okay, here is the time, here is when I can sleep, here's when I can rest, this is what I can do to rest,' Evans says.

'Sitting on your bed, put your pajamas on because then no

one can ask you to go downstairs because you've already got your pajamas on. Do that straight away.' He laughs.

'I've got my book or my music, check the race book, make some notes, maybe check some messages from home. I tried to be quite independent and autonomous about the whole thing and ignore the rest.'

Autonomy in cycling can be a good thing and a bad thing. Feeling comfortable and supported at BMC went a long way to helping Evans manage and then overcome challenges that the environment of the Tour presents.

But when I ask Evans if that feeling of being treated like, or as less than, an animal at the Tour was his biggest challenge, surprisingly, he says no.

'That's part of it and adds to the pressure and expectation that you have but you also have a lot of pressure and expectation from your competitors, from your team, and then of course you have that from the media as well,' he says.

But like Captain Cook, where others had failed, Evans stayed motivated.

'I'd gotten to a point where I'd given so much of my career, I dedicated so much of my time, life, energy, but I'd also made so many sacrifices to get there, to give up would have been cutting myself short,' he says.

CHAPTER 12
MASTER AND APPRENTICE

The sun had long set on Paris when David Brailsford casually raised a glass to Richie Porte, hours after their Sky team had won the 2015 Tour de France with Chris Froome.

Porte had signed with American Jim Ochowicz's BMC squad for the following year and would have the opportunity to compete for the yellow jersey himself, after riding so successfully for Froome and Bradley Wiggins.

Into the night at a private function Brailsford made a short speech, recognising Porte's contribution to the team and wishing him well. Porte, a tanned, 1.72-metre all-rounder, stood up on the sofa bench he'd been sitting on in the darkened room and acknowledged the sentiment, saying something to the effect of, 'If it doesn't work out, I'll be back in two years.'

Two years is a standard contract in cycling, but Porte would be gone for a lot longer and learn a great deal about the type of person he did and did not want to be, and how quickly friend can become foe in pursuit of the *maillot jaune*.

Porte previously had built a reputation as a successful week-long stage racer, time trialist and a hardy super *domestique* in Grand Tours, not just at Sky but at Saxo Bank before that, where he rode for the likes of Alberto Contador.

Porte's teammates at Saxo Bank used to call him 'Fish' because of an aerobic capacity that apparently allowed him to hold his breath for a long time underwater.

He was a loyal teammate, maybe too loyal, he considers now, and never, despite his own clear physical talent had a problem racing for others over himself at the Tour, until a big money opportunity presented itself.

'Going into the race I knew what my job was, and I understood that. I never really had a problem with [the fact] you're there for one person,' Porte says. 'With cycling, the road always works out the pecking order anyway and I was just lucky that I did work for great guys like Froomey or Wiggins, Contador, who nine times out of ten finished it off.'

Froome and Porte developed a close rapport at Sky. They both lived in tax haven Monaco, on the French Riviera, where they trained together and developed a sense of community that included other teammates.

In his first innings at the Tour with Sky, Porte was what Robin is to Batman. It was a role he came back to with the team in 2021, content on seeing out his career racing at Grand Tours under less pressure.

It was easier being Robin, he says, having a finish line on any given stage just short of the actual end of the race. His role was to be good enough to consistently stay with and help his team leader, Batman, at crunch time, and also inflict pain on the rest of the peloton, and in doing so weaken rival contenders and their respective teams.

'It's like now when you see guys like Carlos Verona come up and ride for [Alejandro] Valverde or [Miguel Ángel] López and do almost a max effort, which explodes [the bunch], because they're good bike riders, and that's what I was doing,' says Porte.

'It was almost like [being] a battering ram on the climbs for Froomey.

'That's much easier to do that, empty yourself, and the leader still has to get themselves to the finish, which is so much harder to do.

'At Mont Ventoux, you're finished by four kilometres before the summit whereas that extra four kilometres is mentally huge. It feels like a much longer distance.'

Having driven over Mont Ventoux at the 2021 Tour, I can tell you the last bit of the climb is virtually vertical. There is no grassy moss, just stone all around. It feels like you're on the moon and navigating the summit is a challenge even in a four-wheel drive.

'You've got the pressure, and everyone else's expectations on your shoulders,' Porte continues. 'You still have to do all the work and turn up in great shape but, mentally, it's just miles away from having that pressure of having to do it yourself.'

Porte and Froome are similar in some respects. The Antipodeans both come from non-traditional cycling nations, are gifted and arguably took the hard road to the top.

There is no easy way in elite sport but there is an easier way, which Porte wasn't privy to.

He wanted to be a part of the Tasmanian Institute of

Sport and the Australian Institute of Sport, which run well-funded and highly successful pathway programs, but he was never invited.

'Yes, I've ridden for the best teams now. But I didn't ever have the support of the AIS or the TIS, and I'm not even a part of the TIS now. I was just never part of that boys' club, and that's what it is,' he says.

Porte is a proud Tasmanian and first started cycling on a borrowed bike as a teenager growing up in Launceston, which he returns to every off-season to see his parents. They still answer phone numbers they don't know, including mine the morning in 2020 after Porte, at thirty-six, finished third on general classification behind Tadej Pogačar and Primož Roglič, two faces of a new generation that has become the benchmark in Grand Tour racing.

Pogačar was twenty-one – Porte at the same age had done one year as an amateur.

'He didn't start until late so that's really the amazing thing,' Porte's mother, Penny, said after staying up until about 4 am to see her son stand on the podium in Paris.

Porte came through the domestic scene, racing under the guidance of small team owners Andrew Christie-Johnston and Steve Price, rather than academy squads, but he made the same sacrifices, eventually moving from insulated and isolated Australia to Europe where he competed against AIS counterparts.

'I was doing the races in Italy that they were doing and beating them … and for some reason they had no interest in me. I don't know what I did but obviously I upset someone,' Porte ventures.

'I know I probably shouldn't say some of this stuff, but that's my opinion. That's how I feel, they never had any interest in me.'

It's ironic that Sky, now Ineos Grenadiers, the WorldTour team that most felt like home to Porte, had roots in Britain's imperious academy equivalent.

Porte scored his best result at the Tour in 2020 with the Trek–Segafredo team and then decided to rejoin Ineos Grenadiers on a two-year deal that would see out the rest of his racing days. He planned in advance to retire at the end of the 2022 season of his own volition.

But even now as one of the best stage racers there is, and only the second Australian behind Cadel Evans to finish on the podium at the Tour de France, Porte has a modest view of himself that can perhaps be partly attributed to his rearing in the sport.

'If I stepped back and looked at the races I've won through my career, if it was someone else, I'd be like, other than I haven't won a stage of a Grand Tour, which is something when everyone is so focused on those Grand Tours, but when you're in cycling and you've won the races I have, I'd say that's a hitter,' Porte says.

'But I don't really look at myself as that.

'I've never, I don't know, what would you say, what would you say, Gemma?' he yells out to his wife, who is in the background as we speak over the phone in the European summer of 2021, days after he has won the Criterium du Dauphiné, a litmus test for the Tour.

'I do have the *palmares* [record of achievements] now of a seriously good bike rider, but I've always underestimated myself. I don't have that confidence in myself. I've always been the little guy.'

Porte wasn't a novice when it came to racing as a Grand Tour title contender.

At the end of his first tenure at Sky, which ran from 2012 to 2015, the team backed Porte for a title bid at Giro d'Italia, which was at the forefront of his mind from the beginning of that season. Even in January he was skin and bone, living like a monk off a diet of yoghurt and berries.

'My skin folds were twenty-three, which was the leanest [then Sky head coach] Tim Kerrison had ever seen. Whereas now I'm up around twenty-seven and at least I have some kind of grunt, which I definitely didn't have back then,' Porte recalls.

Every conversation I had with Porte in the first part of that 2015 season came back to the Giro.

I began to think of Porte like an elastic band, stretching out further and further every month in the lead-up until he reached breaking point and, as elastic does, finally snapped under pressure during the campaign.

Porte entered the Giro as a favourite, having won three stages races – Paris–Nice, Volta a Catalunya and Giro del Trentino – in the lead-up.

But he decided to leave the contest after the fifteenth stage to focus on supporting Froome at the Tour after the *maglia rosa*, the pink leader's jersey, spiralled well out of grasp, partly due to rotten luck.

Porte on stage 10 suffered a late mechanical, which put him on the back foot until compatriot Simon Clarke, who was competing for a different team, offered him a wheel so

Porte could get back into the race. It was a profound display of sportsmanship that later saw both riders penalised because the action, unbeknownst to them, went against UCI rules. Porte copped a fine and a two-minute time penalty for his part, which saw him slip to twelfth place on general classification and more than three minutes behind the race leader Contador. A crash later in the week further impeded Porte's position, before he decided to stop and reboot for the summer.

Porte had grown up watching the Tour, which is broadcast at night and into the wee hours of the morning in Australia, with his family.

'I remember staying up until 2 am with my mum while she was doing the ironing, watching it,' Porte recalls. 'I said that to my mum: "One day, that's what I want to do." But then when I started racing and started getting an absolute kicking I kind of thought, "Oh, I'm not really good enough."'

Porte ultimately was convinced otherwise.

'But then guys like Andrew Christie-Johnston and Steve Price, who had the Praties team, they're not rich guys, they just put all their money into making dreams like mine come true,' he says.

And waving self-esteem aside, he had drive.

'You don't move from Tassie to Italy where you don't speak the language without being driven,' he says.

'I'm not the most confident but at the end of the day I still went from a very comfortable life in Tassie and moved to the opposite side of the world and made it work, made it happen.'

Porte doesn't hesitate when I ask him why he decided to leave a team that he loved, where he met his wife, from Manchester, and transition from working as a super *domestique* at the Tour to competing as a yellow jersey contender himself at a rival outfit.

'Probably money,' he says.

And Porte recognises the privileged position he is now in, having made enough of it. When he retires at the end of the 2022 season as a thirty-seven-year-old he says he'll never have to work a 'proper job' again.

'Jim Ochowicz made me an offer that I couldn't refuse, and BMC was a brilliant team,' he continues.

'You know, if we were talking about leaving the best team to go to the seventh- or eighth-best team in the peloton then maybe you wouldn't do it, but at the time BMC was the second-best team in the peloton, so when the offer was there, and it was so good, it was silly not to go and try do it.'

In his first Tour appearance with BMC in 2016, Porte placed a promising fifth, behind Froome, Romain Bardet, Nairo Quintana and Adam Yates, which you can only assume that his former stable took note of because the next year the gloves came off.

I remember having a conversation with a colleague in the Sky Sports studio in London at the time about Porte and Froome as rivals. At Team Sky Porte had been like an apprentice to Froome; the last man able to climb into the clouds with him, sustain the lung burn from breathing in the razor-sharp, thin air there and position the master for the win. But they had also become friends during their multiple quests together, to the point that Froome is the godfather of Porte's first child.

We questioned whether Porte, if it came down to a man-on-man situation, would be ruthless enough to sideline sentiment and trounce his friend for the win, potentially at the expense of their personal relationship.

Froome, we thought, would not have hesitated. A fact Porte would go on to learn.

'He's just an African, he's got that killer instinct in him. That's why he's so good. It's just like foot on the throat kind of thing,' Porte says.

In 2017 the pair competed against each other in the Dauphiné. Porte was in red-hot form and leading the race going into the final stage. Froome was placed fourth overall and Sky were said to have agreed in a morning team meeting that the race was done, and to settle the score at the Tour.

There were whispers though that Froome apparently had different designs. He perceived BMC as weak and, on the road, it was said, helped to organise and orchestrate an ambush that ultimately saw Porte lose the leader's jersey.

It made no difference to Froome or Sky's result in the Dauphiné – they still didn't win – but it sent a clear message before the Tour: Porte would be granted no favours. All's fair in love and war.

The pair have had private conversations about the incident since, but Froome isn't apologetic when I convey Porte's illustration of him as a ruthless, alpha male competitor.

'I can certainly understand that's how people may see me,' says Froome.

'It goes back to being single-minded about competition.

'And I mean for me, personally, I consider Richie to be a lifelong friend that I've met and made through cycling, but anything that happens on the bike stays on the bike and that's part of competition. That's very much my viewpoint on it.'

Porte considers that maybe if he had the same mindset as

Froome, he would have won more races. Off the bike, Froome remains a friend but, on the bike, Porte can't reconcile with his approach.

'The thing is, Froomey and I are wired totally different,' Porte says.

'As a bike rider I admire the guy, how hard mentally he is and what he's been through. The amount of abuse that, whatever you think about Froomey, he did not deserve all the boos and crap he had to put up with. It was unwarranted.

'But at the same time,' Porte counters, 'if someone had dedicated themselves to me for so many years, I wouldn't go out of my way to make sure they didn't win bike races, or the Dauphiné in 2017.

'I've had that conversation with him face to face, he knows my feelings.'

Brailsford once commented that when it came to Porte and the Tour his weakness wasn't physical, it was mental. And my view is that Sky at the ensuing 2017 Tour exploited that.

At the team's pre-race press conference that year, Froome and Brailsford sat at the centre of a long table, flanked either side by the rest of the squad, dressed in casual team kit.

When journalists started asking about the in-form Porte the ensemble, including the usually affable Geraint Thomas, delivered the same, almost rehearsed answer with cold, stony faces: it was Porte's Tour to lose.

That was bullshit.

At his own press conference, Porte recognised the rhetoric for what it was – a mind game designed to add pressure to his shoulders in what was only his second concerted effort as a Tour title contender.

But, to a degree, you could say it worked.

During that Tour, I was mingling at the back of the peloton as it lined up behind the start line of a stage. Porte rode over to me and motioned for my TV cameraman to leave.

'Give us a minute,' I told the cameraman, who obliged.

It was early in the day but already hot and the peloton was just under a week into the race and still nervous. The pecking order had not quite been established.

Porte was dressed in the bright red and black kit of his BMC team, with his glasses off, despite the glare from the sun.

I was working for television that year and a typical day would involve filming at the stage start, and then, after the riders rolled out, driving to the finish. During the drive we'd sometimes have limited communications on what was unfolding in the race, not having race radio and being unable to rely on reception one hundred per cent of the time in rural France. So, you'd be playing catch-up when you finally arrived at your truck in the TV compound.

The day before, I had just got to the truck and watched on the small TV inside as BMC did a load of work on the front of the peloton. I'd posted a question on Twitter, asking why they were working when the onus should have, could have, would have been on the defending champions, Sky.

Porte took issue with me over the tweet.

'You don't understand,' he said with a mixed expression of hurt and anger before riding off.

And, apparently, I didn't. My post wasn't a criticism of him, or his team. It was a genuine question about a race scenario that didn't make sense to me.

I wasn't the only one to ask, either. But I later did something

I should not have and shot back at Porte in a text message when I returned to my hotel that day after the stage, not realising the late hour. It needlessly exacerbated the situation. BMC's press officer mediated and the next day, Porte, when he spoke to me on camera, avoided eye contact while taking aim at journalists who had questioned BMC's tactics.

It all simmered down but was no less a crack in the armour, which days later, during stage 9, was totally exposed when Porte crashed out on a high-speed descent and broke his collarbone and pelvis.

I couldn't have imagined having an interaction like that at the Tour with Froome. That's not to say Froome was any more or less susceptible to such commentary, but he had a different way of channelling it in the moment, which was not to the detriment of his performance.

'For me personally,' Froome says, 'I feel as if when I've worked that hard for something I'm not going to let a bunch of hot noise on the sidelines change anything.

'When you've worked so hard for something you almost learn to block everything else out that's irrelevant to the result.

'That's how it's felt for me over the years,' he continues. 'If it's media, whatever it is, if it's not something that's happened in the race – actually changing the overall standings – then it doesn't really feature on my list of priorities.'

Porte had become the face of the Tour in Australia but the harsh realities and untold pressures of being a title contender were something he had to learn to manage, and it wasn't easy.

The next year at the 2018 Tour Porte started again as an in-form title contender. He entered the race on the back of victory at the Tour de Suisse and on stage 3 BMC showed their collective strength, winning the team time trial ahead of Sky. Porte's teammate Greg Van Avermaet donned the yellow jersey for a stint after the stage win and things appeared to be going well but Porte still felt the heavy pressure that came with his position.

It was such that when he crashed again on stage 9 of the 2018 edition and fractured his collarbone, about 10 kilometres into the 156.6 km run from Arras to Roubaix, before a sequence of cobblestone sectors tipped to bring some title contenders unstuck, he felt one, overriding emotion. Relief.

'I was in the back of the ambulance, and it was like, well, I don't have that pressure on me now, I've got a broken collarbone,' he confesses.

'And you're like the first person I've said that to, but, you know, it's like you had all that pressure and personal expectation of "I just won Tour de Suisse", and coming in as one of the favourites, and we'd just had [son] Luca and I'd hardly seen him, and I wasn't really that happy within BMC at that time.

'I was not in the best place,' Porte continues.

'And then it's just like that, you crash out, you're in the back of the ambulance on the way to hospital and it's almost like, "Thank god that that's happened." It wasn't my fault the crash happened.

'It was almost like running away from a fight.'

Porte returned to the fight in 2019 with Trek–Segafredo, and buried his stage 9 demons, finishing eleventh overall.

He has an acerbic tongue, but he didn't grow fangs or learn to tread on throats prior to his more successful, podium-finishing 2020 Tour campaign. He was not any more or less ruthless.

If anything, he'd chilled out. Setbacks no longer threatened his resolve, or his performance.

'Of course, it is a bit of a maturity thing,' Porte says. 'And then also having my wife, [she] is from Manchester and people from Manchester will say it how it is.

'I have regular conversations with my psychiatrist back in Launceston about things on and off the bike but then Gemma will sometimes read me the riot act.' Many cyclists now consult with sports psychiatrists and psychologists as part of their general performance strategy, working on everything from anxiety over results, to time management, and thrashing out personal issues which may encumber them.

'Having two kids as well, it's not like I come home and the washing and stuff like that does itself, or the dishwasher,' Porte continues.

'You do have a little bit more ...' He searches for the word, 'I'd say responsibilities, but you also have ...'

'Perspective,' I offer.

'Exactly, that's the word, perspective.

'I was never the guy that was buying [a] Rolex – ah, actually – well, watches and Ferraris,' he continues. 'But now you look at some of the stuff you've accumulated over your career, and it just doesn't matter, does it, compared to kids. I'm thinking more about how to put my kids through school now and I think that's the perspective that you need to be a better bike rider.'

The 2020 season started as usual at the Tour Down Under. Coronavirus had barely made the news and toilet paper, which people months later would clear supermarket shelves of, was still in ready supply.

In Adelaide Porte spoke about competing at the Tour, but in more general than concerted terms, and wouldn't then, or at any point during his career-best campaign, put a number on what success would look like.

The postponed 2020 Tour, which he entered as a co-leader opposite Dutch cyclist Bauke Mollema, was fraught with danger, running amid the pandemic. Even the Olympic Games had been called off.

To compete, Porte also had to make the great personal sacrifice of missing the birth of his second child, Eloise.

It served as motivation, and he managed in global chaos to find the eye of the storm. Froome and Thomas were not selected, so there was no, or less, chance of pre-emptive mind games, or old, inhibiting grudges, in my view, and stringent protocols to protect the health of riders significantly limited the access and the number of fans and journalists on the ground, reducing the noise that Porte used to switch off social media to avoid.

Porte rooms alone at races but started to lean on teammates and accept their help and reassurance, which he hadn't always done or felt before. He says former world champion Mads Pedersen became his psychiatrist off the bike, and the closer the team got to Paris, the more they rallied together.

'That's what I needed,' Porte says. 'Mads would come to my room and be like, "All right, tomorrow is not going to be your thing, it's going to be crosswinds, it's going to be hectic, but you're going to be right because I'm going to be behind you or in front of you and Toms [Skujinš] is there as well and Jasper [Stuyven]."

'Almost like I needed my bodyguards.'

That Tour was the start of a renaissance for Porte, not just at Trek–Segafredo but also when he returned to Ineos Grenadiers.

Porte employed the same perspective and resolve coming into the 2021 season with stronger shoulders to handle pressures and unlucky setbacks he once may have cracked under.

He worked in tandem with Thomas in the lead-up to the Tour, notably winning the Criterium du Dauphiné, with the aid of the Welshman, for the first time. With that win, Porte joined Eddy Merckx as the only riders to have won Paris–Nice, Volta a Catalunya, Tour de Romandie, Tour de Suisse and the Dauphiné – a fine collection of traditional, week-long stage races.

'I think I can still take it,' he says. 'The last stage of the Dauphiné was pretty stressful, and I didn't explode.'

I hear Gemma in the background.

'Capitulate, Gemma said, like I could have done in the past. I just dealt with it,' Porte continues.

'You know, I broke my bike, I changed that. I did a technical descent on a bike with a broken shifter, like, I just cracked on with it. And then I fumbled my Garmin and lost that. I know you don't need a computer to win bike races, but you do rely on that as a kilometre marker, power meter to gauge your efforts.'

Porte hardly had time to celebrate what was the biggest stage-race victory of his career, with the Tour so close on the horizon, but it was sweet. He again faced Froome at the Dauphiné, but the tables had turned. Porte this time spearheaded Ineos Grenadiers and Froome was competing for Israel Start-Up Nation.

'The Dauphiné was a race I always wanted to win. I think

it's probably that and Paris–Nice and Tour de Suisse, outside of the Grand Tours, are the ones to win, so to finally come back and do it was a great feeling,' says Porte.

'And at the same time, to do it with this team, which is probably the team that made it so difficult in 2017 when, I guess it's the old swings and roundabouts, or karma even that these were the guys that, well, some of the guys were the guys that made it impossible for me to win it in 2017.'

Evans once said he would never be able to ride for someone else, having competed as a leader at the Tour for so long. Porte was the opposite. He was clear on the 2020 Tour being his last as a contender and his desire to return to the race in 2021 as a super *domestique* before retirement.

However, when we speak on the phone days after his Dauphiné triumph, when Porte has returned home to Monaco, I can't help but ask if he is tempted to give the yellow jersey another crack at the 2021 Tour, given the success he's enjoyed in the twilight of his career.

He's not.

The 2020 Tour was different, Porte says. He was paid to shoulder the pressure that comes with being a contender. The result for him and his family that year was as good as a win.

'I never won the Tour, but I'm happy with my career and how it's panned out,' he says.

Even though Porte knows he can handle the pressure now, he doesn't want to, and you can hear it in his voice as he talks about the night the 2021 Dauphiné finished.

Porte and the team were staying in a nice chalet, had dinner and one glass of wine before Brailsford launched into a team discussion about Tour tactics that lasted until almost midnight.

Brailsford had started by providing Porte feedback about his performance.

'He, in one breath, said to me, "You spend too much time worrying about what's going to happen. You were worried about what's going to happen on the Joux Plane, and you were worried about what was going to happen on the descent of the Joux Plane,"' Porte recalls.

'He's like, "You're wasting energy on stuff that doesn't happen."'

The conversation then turned to the Tour.

'And then he starts, like, talking about, "Yeah, you know, what about if you did this with [Richard] Carapaz and this with Tao [Geoghegan Hart]."

'It's just like, fucking hell, no wonder I've got all this stuff in my head. Throw seven different scenarios at us.

'I was just like, well, you kind of signed me not to take pressure. G [Thomas] deserves one year of at least having a full team behind him [at the Tour], doesn't he? I think.'

Still, Porte reconnoitred key mountain stages in the Alps with Thomas instead of going straight home after it finished.

And at the Tour during pre-race press conferences, he was presented as one of four potential leaders alongside Thomas, Carapaz and Geoghegan, each speaking to media separately via a video link. Whatever he said there, another yellow jersey campaign was not what he had signed up for despite the rich vein of form he and Thomas had harmoniously enjoyed in the lead-up, taking it in turns to win stage races.

'When we signed this contract, I was like, I don't want that pressure anymore,' Porte says.

'I don't think I'm a bad person, Sophie, but when I get

stressed, I am quite prickly, and I am stressed one hundred per cent of the time.

'Everything plays on your mind. You're going through those scenarios of "What if?", and then in a sport like cycling you can't control anything really.

'I'll be a better teammate, a better person if I don't have all that stress and pressure on me.'

When Porte came full circle at the 2021 Tour, he appreciated even more what he had achieved standing on the podium the year before.

At the beginning of the 2022 season Porte announced that he would compete at the Giro d'Italia, not the Tour de France in his final year as a pro cyclist. The team guided him that way.

'I didn't enjoy my Tour last year and to be quite fair it's not the race where you want people that aren't enjoying themselves,' Porte says.

'I just want to try and enjoy my last year, which the team are totally good with.

'But I also got what I wanted out of the Tour in 2020 when I podiumed. That was something I was always striving for and then to finally get it I don't feel like I have that much business with the Tour. Yeah, sure, I would have loved to have won an individual stage, but I can retire happy having not done that.'

CHAPTER 13
BREAKING POINT

After Caleb Ewan crashed out of the 2021 Tour, he said it was a year's work wasted, not one month, or even six. Speaking before the World Championships in October, even though he was looking forward to the season ending, he was also already thinking about the next campaign.

The journey to the Tour has as many ebbs and flows as the race itself and is perhaps why racers insist on continuing even when it borders on illogical.

'I think I did my first Tour de France after four years professional,' Michael Matthews says. 'It was quite a long wait to do the Tour de France and to be honest it was definitely different to what I had expected.'

Matthews was a decorated racer when he made his Tour debut in 2015. He'd won stages of the Giro d'Italia and Vuelta a España and worn the leader's jersey in both.

But when he crashed on stage 3 of the Tour and broke four

ribs, he questioned whether the race that he used to aspire to as a kid was for him.

'I was thinking after that experience that I would never come back to the Tour de France; it was not my race,' Matthews says. 'I just had so much bad luck in it that I thought it wasn't going to be for me.'

There are many instances, which I've mentioned before, of riders continuing in the Tour despite being seriously injured. If it were any other event, they confess, even the Giro or the Vuelta, that type of injury would be grounds to withdraw, no question.

But at the Tour there's this impetus to get back on the bike and keep going. The riders are even celebrated for continuing when it makes more sense to stop.

The first stage of the 2021 Tour was marred with two main crashes, one of which became a bigger headline than the race itself when a spectator holding out a banner overstepped and caused a mass pile-up. Her sign dedicated to her grandparents clipped Tony Martin, who went down, and the peloton fell like dominos around him.

Movistar's Marc Soler had been positioned towards the front and was one of the riders most severely impacted in the crash. After the stage, his team issued a press release detailing how its riders went.

'The Tour de France again honoured its macabre legend' the statement opened with.

Soler had broken both of his arms in the crash. His team said he suffered from acute pain in his right wrist and wasn't able to properly steer his bike to finish.

'Yet,' the statement continued, 'was still able to finish

the stage, almost half an hour behind stage winner Julian Alaphilippe.'

Whoever wrote the press release did a great job. The intro was something wordsmiths would envy and supported the myth and awe that surrounds the Tour. The macabre legend.

After the first stage had finished and Soler was properly assessed it was determined he'd fractured the radial heads in both arms and sustained a separate fracture to the ulnar head in his left arm. His elbows were stuffed, basically.

Now I'm not an expert in this field. Movistar is a big team with big aims and responding to that crash would have been akin to working on the frontline. The Tour de France never stops. It can't. The focus would have been triage, get to the finish if you can and assess from there.

Cycling has a no-needle policy, so instant fixes to mask the pain aren't a thing.

I've contributed to that narrative Movistar so beautifully framed but there is a point – like when you happen upon a rider who physically can't steer their bike because their arms are limp and broken – where glorified suffering becomes outdated. It has in other sports; it has in other races.

But at the Tour, the legend lives on.

Matthews didn't need to prove anything at the 2015 Tour when he broke his ribs. He already had street credit. The World Championships towards the end of the season were also a big objective for him. So, it would have made more sense to abandon and rest, you'd think.

'I don't know if I've told too many people this,' Matthews says.

'I was speaking to our team doctor at the time once I'd

crashed. And he basically said, "Yeah, you have broken ribs but [there's] nothing you can actually do medical wise to fix them, the only thing you can do is let them recover by themselves."'

The doctor advised Matthews that if he was careful, and didn't crash again, he'd be able to get through the Tour, depending on how badly he wanted to.

'He basically said that you have the World Championships, going home now, resting and building up again, you obviously have to start your preparation all over again, so it's best that you continue through the Tour, survive it and then get all the miles for the World Championships at the end of the year,' Matthews recalls.

Riders will tell you that the Tour is the one race that is not used in preparation for something else, but there are exceptions to that rule when a campaign goes wrong. Primož Roglič withdrew from the 2021 Tour, succumbing to crash-related injuries and deciding to reset before the Tokyo Olympics, which worked for him. Geraint Thomas, also injured and with the same objective persevered at the Tour, afraid that if he went home the comedown would be too hard and he wouldn't be able to get back into the zone for the Games.

Matthews, in 2015, however, also had an ulterior motive to continue.

'A side motivation,' he says, 'was to look good for my wedding, which was at the end of that Tour de France.

'I fitted into a really, really nice, fitted Dolce & Gabbana suit because I basically rode the Tour de France and didn't eat for three weeks because it hurt to eat.

'I was the skinniest I've ever been in my entire life, but, man, I looked good on my wedding day.'

They don't call him 'Bling' for nothing.

Matthews finished the Tour and later went on to win silver behind Peter Sagan at the world titles, so pushing through, he reckons, was worth it.

However, the 2015 Tour was a daily slog and Matthews consulted with the team doctor and sports director Matt White regularly.

'Whitey knew what was coming up after and I think he was also hoping I would recover and still be able to achieve something in that Tour de France after he saw what shape I was in,' he recalls.

'There was a lot more days where I was close to stopping than getting through easily.

'The one day that really comes back and rings a bell was a really hard stage, never really big climbs but just undulating all day and the peloton was single file and I was dropped.

'I remember going back to the car and just saying I'm done,' Matthews continues.

'I felt like someone was shoving a knife into my ribs because it was so hard, and I couldn't breathe because every time you breathe your ribs move. So, I was trying to breathe the least amount possible. That was almost killing me it felt like.'

That dogged perseverance can have consequences.

George Bennett believed in Jumbo–Visma's collective goal to see Roglič win the Tour in 2020 so much that he competed from start to finish injured. He doesn't regret doing so but wasn't good again for the rest of the season.

'I was very happy when the Tour was over because I could hardly ride my bike by the end of it, I was absolutely in pieces,' he says.

Simon Clarke believes that a rider's breaking point is when you are competing at less than one hundred per cent fitness, as he was in 2021, finishing in Paris with a fractured L4 vertebra.

'When you're not at one hundred per cent this race can destroy you – literally,' he says.

The 2021 Tour was the hardest Clarke has ever competed in, not because of the different pace or style in which it was contested, rather that he had a hindered run-in and then suffered injuries in a spate of crashes during the opening week.

'As a result, I'm racing at whatever reduced per cent of my capability against guys who are at one hundred per cent. That's where you really suffer,' Clarke explains.

'The guys who you see at the back, take out the sprinters, but the other guys down the lower end of the rankings each day are the guys who are sick or injured and just battling to get through, and that's by far the hardest challenge in Grand Tours in general but particularly in the Tour de France.'

There is a cliché in cycling that 'the Tour is the Tour' and that's about as good an explanation as to why riders push through the pain that you'll get.

'It's cycling's Olympics and every day I line up on the start line I think about the fact this is the Olympics for us, twenty-one days in a row,' says Clarke.

'Although sometimes it feels like, yeah, it does get repetitive, when we retire and look back on it, it's like, to have been able to be a part of cycling history – that is pretty much the Tour de France in a nutshell.

'It's pretty special,' he continues, 'and not everyone is able to do that, or has had the opportunity to. To be able to have done six of them is a pretty big honour.'

In the scenarios where a rider cannot continue it can be devastating for them.

I became so used to riders soldiering on even when injured that when Ewan crashed on stage 3 of the 2021 Tour I waited past the finish line for him, assuming he'd hobble over it eventually.

The peloton beyond the finish line had significantly dispersed when his press officer walked by, and I asked, 'Where's Caleb?'

'Still on the road,' he replied.

When the crash with Sagan occurred, Ewan knew immediately that something wasn't right.

'The weird thing was, usually when you crash you have so much adrenaline that you don't really feel the pain for a while, but I remember sliding on my back feeling my back burning,' he recalls.

But even then, his mind was on the race.

'My initial thought was like, "Damn, I've just lost heaps of points for the green jersey," ' Ewan continues.

'And then about ten seconds after that I was like, "Oh, something is not feeling good," and then I could feel my collarbone clicking.

'I've never broken a bone before, so I didn't know the feeling of a broken bone but then the medical people pressing on it, it was like excruciating pain.'

It was, he says, the lowest point of his Tour career – both the crash and being forced to watch the rest of the race from home.

'I'll watch it and then after I'll be like, "Damn, I could have been there sprinting myself," and that's a hard thing,' Ewan says.

'In the end I am a fan of the sport and I think when you watch lots of sprints there's always something to learn from it as well. Of course, it was hard to watch because I know I could have been there, and it could have possibly been me winning.'

It is the small wins on the road that help injured riders to persevere at the Tour.

I don't mean wins with hands aloft crossing the finishing line to claim a stage victory, but rather markers along the route, which may go unseen but are significant.

As the weeks progress, from first to second and third, the pace in the peloton changes, allowing, as absurd as it sounds, riders opportunities to recuperate.

'Until the first rest day you constantly try, and slowly getting more and more tired and trying to be conscious of not using too much energy where possible,' says Clarke.

'Then I think from the first rest day onwards your body gets so tired that even [a] one-hundred-and-fifty-to-one-hundred-and-eighty-kilometre flat day, where you can take it easy, actually, is pretty much a rest day for your body, and you can recharge the batteries on a day like that.

'You don't notice that until your body gets so tired that you then, on a day like that, actually bounce back,' Clarke continues.

'Basically, from the first rest day onwards it's about trying to pick those days and maximise the active recovery and try and get the batteries back up as high as possible.'

Some people have dubbed time trials for everyone outside of time trial specialists and title contenders as rest days.

In his quest to survive through his Tour debut with broken ribs, Matthews says he was able to take paracetamol, which I can't imagine took the edge off.

He recalls a stage that was ravaged by crosswinds and rains.

'I was the first one dropped and then got back on again, dropped and got back on again,' Matthews says.

He only just survived the stage but, in doing so, won the prize for the most combative rider that day. It's not an accolade that necessarily makes headlines, but it does signify the gutsiest rider of the day. And it gave Matthews a bigger boost than Panadol.

'I was pretty happy just to go back to the bus and start my recovery,' he continues.

'But to go to the podium and grab something from that Tour where I was just struggling every day, and for people to, I guess, appreciate how much pain I was going through and still continuing to fight, was definitely a highlight of that Tour de France, considering there weren't many highlights.'

After questioning whether the Tour was a race for him, Matthews returned the next season and won his maiden stage with surety.

He and the team had done the same stage finish years before and checked it out again on YouTube as a memory refresher.

He can recall the day with crystal clarity as it transformed his perception of the Tour.

'I was a bit scared about the start, twenty kilometres uphill, it was always going to be a crazy start,' he recalls.

'But I had really good legs that day, I put a lot of focus into this stage.

'We started uphill, and I ended up in a group of, I think, five over the top of the first climb in the breakaway.

'I remember coming down the descent, it was really foggy

and Vincenzo Nibali was on the front railing the descent. I could not see five metres in front of me, all I could see was his back wheel and his backend, so I was like, "Okay, as long as I can hold this guy I'll be in the breakaway for the day and hopefully go for the victory, if it's the right breakaway."' Nibali is one of the best descenders in the peloton.

At the bottom of the descent Matthews had spied a group over his shoulder, hoping it wasn't the peloton. And then he spotted two of his teammates, Daryl Impey and Luke Durbridge, amongst it.

'I was like, "Okay, now we're on for a good stage here,"' he continues.

'We had I think twelve to fifteen guys in the breakaway, all really strong, classics riders too. I think Greg [Van Avermaet] was there, Sagan was there, who else, [Edvald] Boasson Hagen was there, a lot of other guys I would have been contesting that stage with anyway if it came to a bunch sprint were also in the breakaway.

'I was thinking, "This is going to be hard, but if I can pull this off it will be really incredible."'

Impey and Durbridge motored to ensure the peloton did not catch the breakaway and Matthews was in the best position to contest the stage win.

'Then on the final climb to the finish there was, I think, two kickers and actually our bunch split in half,' Matthews continues. 'I think we only had maybe seven guys in the front, and we still had three of us in the front, which worked out perfectly again.

'On the final kicker Durbo drove it into the bottom, made sure everyone stayed together and then Impey kept a really good pace over the top where guys were attacking but he kept bringing them back all the time, so set it up for the sprint for me.'

Matthews finished the job, won the sprint from Sagan and Boasson Hagen, and then in the melee past the line at Revel, crushed by photographers and camera crews trying to capture the raw emotion of the moment, looked for his teammates.

'After so many bad experiences in the Tour and so many close calls to winning a stage, getting that first one was something that dreams were made of,' Matthews says.

'I think crossing that finish line I didn't really understand what I just did – achieved. All those memories from being seventeen ... watching it on the TV, to having all the crashes, bad luck, to then pulling that off, especially the way we did it, the team, was even more special than I could have ever imagined, winning my first Tour de France stage.'

Matthews has a colourful nickname – 'Bling' – but a caring and grounded temperament. He doesn't have a poker face and he doesn't play games. When he fails to figure in stages he is fancied for, his clear disappointment is gutting.

At the 2021 Tour Matthews had finished second on the first stage to Landerneau behind Alaphilippe. It gave him confidence for the days ahead, which also suited his characteristics. But then on the next opportunity he didn't figure. Past the finish line he had come to a halt, stooped low over his handlebars, his shoulders drooped. The BikeExchange press officer had looked over at me and shook her head, indicating he may not speak.

Matthews took time to regain his composure and then did come over, but his normally chipper tone was replaced with a low whisper. He later thought that side-effects from a COVID-19 vaccine he received before that Tour may have affected his form in the opening days.

Tour champions get to a point in their careers where they start describing wins there not as the life-changing moments they're sold as, or even fun, but first and foremost a relief. A relief that they've been able to prove themselves, a relief that they've been able to repay the work their teammates had put in with a win, a relief that the sponsors will be happy and continue to fund their team and thus their livelihoods.

Ewan notes the difference from when he made his long-awaited debut in 2019, keen to prove himself after being held back by his former team, to 2021 when he was a poster boy.

'The first one I felt the pressure because I feel like it was a long time coming that I was going to the Tour, and it didn't happen as quick as I'd hoped. And also, I had the thing with Mitchelton where I believed I was ready for it, but they didn't,' Ewan says.

'I felt the pressure like I had the eyes on me that Tour because it was like, all right, if you were good enough, you're going to show us now.

'But it's a different type of pressure now,' Ewan continues.

'I feel like after that Tour I went into the next Tour as one of the favourites of the sprinters, and that's a different type of pressure to handle as a favourite, whereas the first Tour I probably didn't go in as a favourite.

'It was my first Tour so whatever happened, happened. After that, after having a successful Tour, like that year, you're just expected to win and anything else is a disappointment. And if you win, it's just, all right, you're supposed to win.'

Matthews does describe his maiden Tour stage win as a relief but in the moment, when he was barrelling towards the finish line, he was not overcome with emotion, as he sometimes is in defeat, or conscious of the weight of expectation rested on his shoulders.

'I was actually quite calm to be honest,' he recalls.

'Impey was on the front setting a really high tempo that no one would attack, and I think from the guys around me I was quietly confident. I had a super day that day, I don't know what I did the rest day before, but all my stars just aligned on that one day.

'There was a bit of a chicane coming into the finish, like slight downhill after the final climb, then a right-left into the straight, I think it was four hundred metres to the finish from the last corner,' Matthews continues.

'I remember I was on the right, I think I was on Sagan's wheel where he was on Impey's wheel and I think Greg went quite early in the sprint, around two hundred and fifty.

'I could jump onto him and then start my sprint off him.'

Everything just came together for Matthews.

'Once I started my sprint, I knew from that point that it was going to be very difficult for someone to pass me.'

Sports director Matt Wilson was driving in the team car behind the breakaway that day, and at the finish had tears in his eyes.

'You could see how much it meant to him also, that victory,' says Matthews. 'He saw how much I wanted it and did everything to make sure I could put myself in the best possible place to go for that victory. The whole emotion from the whole team was really special.'

Matthews looked at the Tour differently from that moment on.

'All the bad luck I've had in the race, to have one day of good luck it changes your whole thinking about a certain race, your whole outlook about a certain race,' he says.

'Us cyclists, we have selective memories where we really, I can only speak for myself, but I really try and only think about the positive things of certain bike races, or certain things to do with cycling.

'If you only think of the negatives, it's going to be a difficult career.'

CHAPTER 14
SECRETS OF A SOIGNEUR

At the Tour everything possible is done for the riders so that all they must focus on is sleeping, eating and competing. Some days I think the peloton has the easiest gig out of everyone who works there – if you put that small thing of racing down to semantics.

'I never had to think,' Dutch cyclist Boy van Poppel once said to me about his formative years in cycling.

They have chefs, bus drivers, doctors, mechanics, sports directors, coaches and massage therapists. On long transfers to the next stage, which may be a day's drive away, riders will jump on private coaches at a stage finish and be dropped off at the door of a chartered flight waiting on the tarmac. On arrival at their hotel a team staffer will stand in the foyer handing out room keys, saving the competitors from the tenuous aspects of check-in.

On the flip side, there is no alone time at the Tour. Riders are working at a heightened capacity, exposed only to extremes amid a constant cacophony of sound in which most people would probably struggle to think.

This is especially true for the cyclists who stay in twin share accommodation at the race and throughout the season, some spending more time sleeping in the same room as a teammate than with their partner at home.

It's difficult to call home, or phone your sports psychologist, or psychiatrist, and go over something that has affected you at the Tour when you've got seven teammates sitting in close quarters on a bus, or one lying within reach on another king single or double bed mattress.

Mathew Hayman recalls that the teams he competed for tried to ensure the riders who roomed together had complementary personalities because when they were back at the hotel was the only time they could relax.

'You're going through something pretty brutal and then you're with a teammate and that has to click otherwise it can make things worse. If you're not comfortable in that period it's tough and you don't want to be on the phone to your wife complaining about your roommate the couple of hours a day you get to relax,' he says.

In most other international sports, the stage on which you perform does not change – a pitch is always rectangular, the baseline of a tennis court doesn't move. Yet in cycling and the Tour the stage changes dramatically, every day.

When that happens it can be a source of anxiety, an opening for negativity to seep in, especially when you're asked to compete on terrain that goes against your physiology no matter how good your form.

Hayman recalls feeling a sense of foreboding when it came

to psyching himself up on the morning of mountain stages at the Tour.

'There definitely is dread on those days and a feeling of impending doom on the way to the start, and just trying to talk yourself out of that,' Hayman says.

'The finish is never normally the problem, it's normally the first half of the stage that I struggle with. By the time I'm on the last climb I kind of know that I'm going to make it home.'

As the race ground on, fatigue would sink its claws harder into Hayman's shoulders and the foreboding, even with some of the mountainous stages behind him, usually increased.

'By the third week it's battling the fatigue and you're starting to get irritable, you're starting to not sleep, starting to doubt yourself,' he says.

'Getting up in the morning and looking at the [stage] profile and knowing there's a climb out of the start, some of it is just wishing and hoping you've got the legs to follow them, you know.'

To combat the doubt, which can inhibit performance as fast as fire spreads, Hayman began to work with a sports psychologist he'd gone to as an under-19 in Australia.

'We had tactics both for before the race and after the race. I used them in the bus and had different recordings to listen to,' he says.

'I knew it was going to be hard and I made a deal with myself what I was going to do. A lot of that is unnecessary, and you just have to say, "What I'm going to do is what I do every day, and do my very best, and if it's not good enough today so be it. I can't be worried about how fast everyone else is going to ride."'

I've written before about the increasing number of riders in the peloton who seek counsel from sports psychologists and psychiatrists during the year and around big objectives.

At the Tour, from the moment riders wake at dawn, it's work, work, work, until their head hits the pillow again. There's no time to seek private counsel in a quiet place without being overheard, except for a small forty-five-minute-to-one-hour-long window when a rider will leave their hotel room to see a *soigneur* for a massage or treatment after a stage.

It is so loud competing in the peloton at the Tour de France that Hayman used to wear noise-cancelling headphones on the drive from the end of a stage to the next hotel to try and lower his adrenaline levels.

'You've got helicopters above you, you've got a radio in your ear turned up to full volume listening to Whitey [Matt White] talk to you, and it has to be at full because of the noise of the crowd, people shouting, and you're in a bus, in cars. So massage, and when your roommate is getting a massage, and you're in a room by yourself, sometimes you really do hear your ears ringing and realise that's the first time today there has just been no noise, action and adrenaline,' he says.

'By the end of three weeks that's what also makes you tired.

'You're just physically exhausted. I notice it now even as a director, same thing, the crackling of the race radio and the long days, it is absorbing all of that action for three weeks.'

Back at the hotel, on the massage table, the echo of the Tour, of racing in the peloton, would momentarily subside for Hayman.

Every team employs *soigneurs*, or 'swannys', who are part of the support crew and are there to assist the riders. Their role is traditionally as a masseur but has since expanded to cover anything riders need. However, the general description of a *soigneur* belies the true magnitude of their job and the secrets they are trusted with.

They are quasi-therapists to riders, some of whom use the *soigneur*'s treatment rooms as a type of confessional, dropping their shoulders and dumping their concerns once they can finally think in peace and quiet.

Hayman recalls often venting to his *soigneur* during treatments.

'He'd say, "Woah, woah, woah, calm down." And I'm like, "Oh this bloody idiot," and this and that,' Hayman says.

'A lot of the time the *soigneurs* are the sports psychologists of the team.

'What you'd normally be [talking about] with your partner, going over the day and complaining about things, I'd normally talk through with him, and had a pretty good relationship with him.'

Hayman would go over everything that happened during his day, and, at the end of it, feel calmer and more relaxed.

Riders value a good *soigneur*. Michael Matthews personally employed his in 2021, and others will include them as part of their entourage when transferring between teams.

Kurt Van Roosbroeck is a physiotherapist and when he's not on the road with Deceuninck–Quick-Step for 170 days of the year, he runs his own practice at home in Belgium.

'I always do one massage of a rider. And then depending which rider needs some extra therapy, then I do my job as a physiotherapist,' Van Roosbroeck says.

At the 2021 Tour, in which Quick-Step won five stages and the green jersey, Roosbroeck did massage for Kasper Asgreen. Prior to his arrival at the team, he worked with the likes of Jürgen Roelandts and Cadel Evans at Lotto.

'Towards the end of the Tour a lot of riders start to complain about back pain, neck pain, pelvic pain, you know, because of the stages, three weeks in a row,' he says.

'Sometimes when a rider crashes, we need to do a check-up of the static and then I do my treatment as a physio, so the correction of the pelvis, I make some therapy on the muscles on the neck, whatever they need.'

Van Roosbroeck grew up playing football but was introduced to cycling by chance. Fifteen years later it is his passion for the sport that has kept him on the road, treating the physical ailments of riders at races and listening to them.

At the Tour *soigneurs* will take over a hotel room to do their treatments. You can tell where they are because the door is usually left slightly ajar and there is a faint whiff of something like Dencorub or Deep Heat that carries through the corridor.

They will push the bed in the hotel room to one side, hoping not to find anything nasty underneath. Hotels at the Tour range from five-star to feral and everyone experiences both. At the 2021 edition one *soigneur* found a bunch of empty condom wrappers under a bed he moved to make space for a massage table.

ASO is in charge of assigning hotels to teams and, due to the nature of the event, they can't all be glamorous, not even for winners like Evans.

'I remember one year we had a rest day at a hotel in the

Pyrenees and the swimming pool was full of concrete rubble, they were renovating the hotel,' says Evans.

'It had this big pool, but it didn't have any water in it. It was full of the building that they had pulled down next door. This is the rest day of the Tour de France.'

One of the biggest misconceptions about the Tour is the accommodation. You do sometimes stay in some magical places, but the majority of it doesn't match the majesty of architecture shown on TV. It is what it is sometimes.

'You know what, as long as the sheets are clean, it's not noisy and I have a decent meal, I'm actually okay because it's better than sleeping in a tent,' says Evans.

'Any hotel is better than a tent. Normally. Almost.'

Van Roosbroeck will usually work with Asgreen and Iljo Keisse if he's at the same race as them. They have an open dialogue.

'Everybody in the team, the *soigneurs* and me as a physio, with some riders it's normal you have a closer connection than with other ones,' he says.

'For example, when Kasper is in the race, he always comes to me for a massage. And then I have the same connection with Iljo Keisse.

'With those two guys I speak more about, let's say, some private things than I would speak with other riders, but when they enter the room, and they go on my table to start the massage, or the treatments, they need to start the conversation,' he says.

Van Roosbroeck has made it a personal rule when he's working at the Tour that the riders he treats must initiate conversation first.

'I start my massage and when the rider starts to speak, no matter about which subject, I will repeat him, and then we start the conversation, but I will never start myself the conversation,' says Van Roosbroeck.

'That's how I work.

'Some days, a rider wants to have the quietness, he doesn't want to speak, he wants to just rest, he wants to be on his own and just enjoy the massage,' he continues.

'And some days, yeah, they want to speak about their frustrations, problems they have. Some days it happens that they tell me a lot, but some days it can also be possible there is maybe three words which are said.'

Van Roosbroeck admits his approach might sound crazy, but it helps him to ascertain the mood of the rider he is treating and allows them to set the subject because sometimes they don't want to talk about the Tour.

'That's, for me, important – that hour, with me or another *soigneur* – the rider, maybe that's the only hour during a day that the rider can have complete rest if he wants because there is no sports director who wants to talk about the tactics, there is no media, no journalists who can ask him something, it's just you and the rider,' Van Roosbroeck says.

Matt Rabin is a chiropractor and head of physical therapy at EF Education–EasyPost; a regular at the Tour, he knows not to ask the riders how they are feeling.

Rabin, like Van Roosbroeck, wakes up at around dawn to do daily exercise. It's the only time he and his colleagues have during the day to look after their own physical wellbeing.

'If you're doing exercise you have to get it done before anyone is around,' he says.

'My work is largely contact with the riders. They all tend to sleep in, so I try and get up super early before anyone is at breakfast.

'I like to go for a walk or go for a run first thing, so you get your physical exercise, movement, done because if you're on the Tour you can travel four hundred to five hundred kilometres a day but not move your body more than five hundred metres. It just does my head in.'

Once the riders are at breakfast Rabin will drop in and see them.

'Literally just stick my head around the door, not even ask … questions because if you ask people how they're feeling you get generally, "I feel like shit,"' Rabin says.

He knows that if the riders want him, they'll call out.

At the stage start Rabin will be on the bus.

'There will be one or two guys who will either need some work on the bus, some movement stuff, some stretching stuff, some mobility stuff,' he says.

'One or two guys might want to get taped up, one or two might be a bit stiff from travel because it can be anywhere from a kilometre to one hundred kilometres to the start of the race.'

Once the race rolls out his responsibilities change. Sometimes he'll go straight to the finish and other times he will help the *soigneurs* out along the route.

Aside from pre-race and post-race treatments, *soigneurs* do everything in between.

One of Rabin's colleagues, a certified physiotherapist, Paul Navin, is almost impossible to track down and get a minute with at the 2021 Tour, he is that busy.

'Our main responsibility is to make sure that the only thing the guys need to focus on is riding their bike,' says Navin. 'So, everything else is taken care of, if it's food, drinks, being picked up at the airport, being dropped off at the airport, if they have letters to post, if they have toiletries to buy, basically all of that.'

At the Tour the *soigneurs* will also do laundry. They prepare musette bags filled with snacks, and bidons, then stand on the roadside by feed zones ready to sling them to the riders, who motion for one as they cycle past at designated points during stages.

'We also prepare food for all of the staff on the race, clean the cars, and then anything else in between, so if the car needs to be serviced or if someone needs to go to the hospital, if someone needs to be driven somewhere,' says Navin.

Navin is one of five *soigneurs* at his team and during the 2021 Tour they split into different groups.

He would be with the first group at the stage starts and finishes, ready and waiting to immediately provide whatever his riders needed. Then later back at the hotel, he would also do massage.

The *soigneurs* gather around with the media just past the finish line to watch the end of every stage on TVs placed under small, white marquees. The second the peloton crosses the line they've mobilised, turning on their heels to look for their people, who will usually ride straight to them first – win, lose or draw.

The condition of the riders depends on the stage, and you never know what you'll get.

If it's a cold day in the mountains the *soigneurs* will carry warm clothes that the riders can put on before they turn to find the team bus, preventing their lips from turning blue.

American Sepp Kuss, wrapped in a scarf, still shook from the cold, his lips a funny tinge, when he spoke to me briefly, managing a smile, on one of the coldest, greyest, wintry days of the 2021 Tour.

On a hot day at the end of a bunch sprint, there may be extra bidons, small cans of soft drink and Haribo lollies pulled out of team-issue backpacks, which are loaded to the brim with supplies. Peter Sagan is partial to Haribo and will shovel the lollies into his mouth like a kid until his cheeks expand.

On a day of carnage and chaos, it's different again. The *soigneurs* may walk with a rider who can't physically pedal further to the bus, or give them a push and direct them to where it is parked.

'Then we have the second group who just go from hotel to hotel each day,' Navin continues.

'So, we'll have two people who take the riders' luggage, set up the hotel for the end of the stage so everything is ready when they get there. And then another group is to do the feed [zone], so two people will do the feed [zone].'

With the stage finished and everyone back at the next hotel, Rabin will triage who he needs to see first.

'If there had been a crash you'd see them first typically, once the doc has patched them up and stuff, and then going through the riders who need it,' he says.

'Out of the eight riders we have, I might see four or five of them an evening, you might have an evening when you see all of them, you might have an evening where you only see two or three of them. It kind of varies.'

Rabin doesn't do massages. His practice revolves around mobility work and activation exercises, and in the interest of efficiency and wanting to get everything done before dinner, he will work in tandem with the masseurs.

'When they [riders] have their massages, usually four guys will be on massage, four guys will be in their rooms. So, I'll try and jump through the four guys who are in their rooms first, try and get those done and then they'll swap over, and I'll jump in on the guys who have had massage and talk to them about stuff, their day, injuries, how the race went,' he says.

Rabin can spend a lot of one-on-one time with the riders and over the course of the Tour naturally builds a rapport with them.

'I suppose it's a bit like being the priest; they just sort of tell you all sorts of shit that's going on in the race, in their lives, whether it be a contract situation, you hear all these different stories, nuances,' Rabin says.

'Often times it's them mouthing off, it's them moping about other riders in the peloton, just hearing those stories. I might know another rider in the peloton that they've had a situation with, and I might reach out to them, if you like, if they've asked me to, or implied they want me to diffuse a situation. That's happened a few times.'

The riders may also vent about internal team tactics.

'Whereby a rider will think that they've got good legs and the team should be riding for them and they're going better than the leader, and so they'll be pissed about that,' Rabin continues. 'If a team at the start of a race says, 'Okay, we're riding for x and then rider y is like, "Well, I'm going better than them, why are we riding for them?"'

Today's generation Rabin believes are 'lower maintenance' than the champions who paved the way before them.

'Back in the day when you had your Davids [David Millar] and your Christians [Christian Vande Velde], these guys, we'd be working until, like, dinner and then still working until 11 to 11.30 pm quite commonly,' he says.

'I would say it doesn't happen as much anymore because they're just like, dare I say, they're not kids, but they're just so much more respectful of the staff.'

When it comes to treatments, Rabin works to a similar ethos as Van Roosbroeck in that he allows whoever is on the table to dictate the rhythm of conversation.

In his experience the room can be like a kitchen party, where one person is getting treated and a handful of others are listening to music and hanging out. Other times, it's the opposite.

'You have to manage that stress because sometimes they just want to kick off, sometimes they want to throw their toys out the pram,' he says.

'You need to get to them to the bigger picture, you need to get them to see the next race is there, you need to get them to understand what it is to be a team player and that your legs won't be wasted, this kind of thing.'

There's lots Rabin has heard and would never divulge but there are other instances where saying something to someone has helped a situation. A large part of it, he says, is emotional intelligence.

'For me, doing your hands-on skills as a chiropractor, to try and change pain, improve function, make them feel more comfortable on the bike, that is an absolute bare minimum requirement,' Rabin says.

'But then it's having the soft skills to communicate with

them, get them to really open up about what their problem is, if you like.

'And the Tour de France is a long race. I remember many times over the years, you're literally trying to keep that rider's head on for three weeks because his head is gone, or he's pissed off about something, and you can't be the rider who goes against the team.

'It's not really chiropractic.'

Not everyone needs to hear the sound of silence at the Tour, but recovery is important.

Marcel Kittel, similar to Evans, found the rigmarole around fame, being pushed and pulled in different directions, doing the rounds with media and shaking hands with sponsors ate into his recovery time. Stage winners and jersey leaders must every day at the Tour fulfil a round of media and sponsorship obligations.

'Fame is one thing but real work after you, for example, win a stage, talks with the media and all the interviews that you have to give I think that's something that really has an impact on the rider,' Kittel says.

'It takes sometimes an hour until you are done with everything, then you need to do a doping control, then you need to drive back to your hotel, it's really interrupting your whole recovery period after a race, and we're talking about the hardest sports event in the year, in general. Every hour counts there.'

He partly attributes those interruptions to having to abandon the 2017 Tour.

'When I had to walk around there after the stage, and not being able to just go back into my bus and just sit there and eat and take a shower and recover, and on top of that you also shake hands, there is a risk to get sick suddenly,' he says.

But winning and celebrating with teammates generally countered the stress.

'It's a moment where you get rid of a lot of pressure that you can share and enjoy with your teammates together,' Kittel says.

'You don't really always have alone time necessary for it but also with a victory sometimes it's nice to sit somewhere quiet and have a moment for yourself.'

In his last Tour in 2018 there was a day Kittel blew up, having failed to figure in a bunch sprint. He didn't stop as he crossed the line, powering straight to the team bus where, in one swift movement, he dismounted from his bike, boarded the coach, and screamed so loud you could hear it from outside. I'd never seen him react to a situation like that before at the Tour. But it's not uncommon either.

'Dealing with a loss, with a defeat, especially in a sprint, it's a moment of pure excitement and also can be very intense, and then when you lose all these negative feelings just come into your head and you have a feeling sometimes you would like to scream,' says Kittel.

'But most of the time you have that for a couple of minutes, and I could always deal with it quite good, or, I had my crazy two minutes in the bus, and would throw a helmet around, or at least on my seat, and try to calm down.'

For Kittel, his teammates served as counsel.

'In the end,' he continues, 'you also deal with it together with your teammates and try to get over it, talk about it, forget about it and turn it into an advantage for the next day, as a motivation to try and go for the victory again and again.'

Van Roosbroeck, similar to Rabin, starts his own day around 6 am with about a 12-kilometre run, and ends with a beer in the team bus with colleagues.

In Van Roosbroeck's capacity as a physiotherapist he may see one rider every day, and another once or twice during the Tour.

His workload ebbs and flows with the race, from the first, nervous, stressful week, where everyone is trying to get chalk on the board, to the third week of competition, where bodies are worn.

'Everybody is tired because you work seven days in a row week after week and then the little, smallest problem becomes sometimes a big problem just because of the fatigue, that you're tired,' he says.

'In the past it was more they were short with you and sometimes screaming, but I cannot say this is happening anymore.' This I would say is true of everyone who works at the Tour. You try and pick who you travel with wisely because it's almost a guarantee that at some point during the race you will fall out, often over something as trivial as turning left when you were meant to go right. I've found over the years that opposites attract and I'm usually best with people whose calm can tame my fire. 'You attract more beers with honey,' Japanese journalist Maki Terao used to remind me.

Riders usually call on Van Roosbroeck more during the third week of the Tour.

Physically, their complaints differ from that of the general public that he treats outside of racing.

'Most of the problems are muscle injuries, when they have a crash and problems with the static – they are blocked in the neck, they are blocked in the lower back, the pelvis goes out of position,' he says.

'More riders ask, "Can you check me because I feel something there," because of the fatigue, and the impact on the body of two weeks and a half of every day of racing.

'They are tired, they're looking forward to Paris, they're counting off the days,' Van Roosbroeck continues.

'Sometimes they're also a little bit more short in their answers, or less jokes but it's just because of the fatigue. Once we arrive in Paris you see everybody forgets the stress, the fatigue and they are the same again, like they just started the Tour.'

CHAPTER 15
ONCE AND FUTURE KING

About an hour before Tadej Pogačar cruised through the penultimate stage of the 2021 Tour de France to all but seal his second consecutive title victory, I'd gone to find his UAE Team Emirates bus.

It was the first really hot day of what was an unseasonably cold Tour and, even in a light cotton dress, I was a sweaty mess by the time I found the white coach with red, green and black detailing, parked on a narrow road, surrounded by team cars, vans and trucks.

The penultimate stage was a 31-kilometre time trial from Libourne to the ancient city of Saint-Émilion, and because of that there was more equipment around at the finish.

A white awning blind, fully extended from one side of the UAE Emirates bus, was shading a group of staff members dressed in black-and-white sneakers, blue jeans and black T-shirts. Team manager Andrea Agostini stood out in his short-sleeved white shirt, which he'd left untucked.

The men were standing, glued to a TV showing Pogačar on the course. Pundits and rivals thought he might go for line honours that day, but Pogačar wasn't in the zone, having just won two consecutive stages in the Pyrenees and boasting a healthy lead on the general classification. His aim was to get through the time trial safely.

As Pogačar crossed the finish line the group erupted. The sound of piercing horns carried across the street as the staff embraced one another with hearty pats on the back and broad smiles you could see even from a distance.

They then gathered in a circle, jumping up and down on the spot, arms aloft as if they were in the mosh pit of a rock concert.

'Hey, hey, hey, hey,' they cheered.

I was standing next to a small crew from American broadcast network NBC.

Allan Peiper was part of the UAE group within shouting distance of us and we yelled out to him. He was who I wanted to see.

Peiper had directed Pogačar to his maiden Tour victory the year before but had largely sat this one out. His happy demeanour in Saint-Émilion, where he'd arrived by popular demand from staff and riders to help bring Pogačar home, belied the fact that he was ill.

The NBC crew got the footage they needed and moved on, leaving me with Peiper.

I knew of his long battle with cancer but not that he was having another big fight with it and that is why he was absent for most of Pogačar's second campaign. Peiper still looks like a bike racer, slender with deeply tanned skin, which contrasts with his white hair.

He asked how my health was, how my mum's health was. She had been diagnosed with and recovered from kidney cancer the year before. My media accreditation lanyard was still around my neck but in that moment I stopped being a journalist.

I said what I could without losing my composure and then changed the subject. 'Genuinely, how are you?' Peiper's voice started to crack, and his eyes started to well, like mine, as he shared. He had every reason to stay at home but instead he was at the Tour to see 'son' Pogačar.

I spotted Bahrain Victorious sports director Rolf Aldag walking over as I tried to pull it together. Aldag and Peiper had previously worked together, and I assumed the German had come to find Peiper and congratulate him on Pogačar's win.

Peiper sobbed as Aldag embraced him. The combination of his own private war and Pogačar's battle for another yellow jersey, which signalled the dawn of a new era at the Tour, was overwhelming.

Peiper regained his composure and talked shop with Aldag as Pogačar, elsewhere, was adorned in another podium ceremony and then prepared for his winner's press conference.

The press conference for the winner of the Tour de France is traditionally held after the penultimate stage each year. The run into Paris the next day is a race for the sprinters but largely ceremonial for everyone else, although some do contest that theory.

The conference was in a small, nondescript arena within a modern building not in keeping with the rest of the town, some of which is UNESCO world heritage listed. I usually would have tried to duck out and see some of that during the stage, but I was so tired that I'm pretty sure I told an ABC radio presenter in a live update from the finish that I was in Libourne not Saint-Émilion.

Pogačar walked into the arena and sat at a rectangular table, which was covered in a black cloth. Behind him was a multicoloured screen showing all the major sponsors of the race.

Plastic chairs had been placed in front of him, spaced about a metre apart, and behind that wood pallets where TV cameras balanced on tripods squarely aimed at cycling's future king.

Pogačar sat comfortably in a long-sleeved yellow jersey, his elbows relaxed on the table, hands together holding a microphone. A yellow mask covered his face and he'd opted for a traditional white cycling cap over a baseball hat, as he waited for the world's media to fire away. His face still has child-like qualities.

It was the first time we'd been in the same room as him. All other press conferences that year had ventured from the traditional script and been conducted via video link due to newly introduced COVID-19 protocols.

In 2020, Pogačar had become the youngest winner of the Tour in 112 years, not that you would have guessed it from his attitude.

Throughout his successful title defence in 2021 he'd addressed the press with a genuine sense of maturity and command beyond his years. He referred to Ben O'Connor, who celebrated a solo victory on the first summit finish in the Alps, as a 'kid', even though the Australian is older than him.

Pogačar's rivals had been beaten into submission long before this penultimate stage, even those at Ineos Grenadiers.

'I don't think he's unbreakable,' Geraint Thomas said during the race. 'But as Dave [Brailsford] would say, he's like bamboo. He bends, but he rarely snaps.'

Pogačar fielded questions about anti-doping in an orderly manner. No, he wouldn't provide his training and performance numbers to satisfy the media he was clean because it would give his rivals an advantage on him, which I thought was fair enough, if not obvious.

He was asked questions in English, which would be later translated into French. A handful of Slovenian journalists waited to speak to him in their native tongue.

Having just come from seeing Peiper, I asked Pogačar to talk about his relationship with the man who, along with Slovenian Andrej Hauptman, had become a self-described guardian to the prodigious talent.

'I first met Allan three years ago in training camp, I had a lot of respect for him and then the first race with him I did in Australia, the one-day classic after Down Under, it was a really great experience I'll never forget,' Pogačar said, recalling his first two races as a neo-pro.

'He taught me a lot, more about life than cycling, and he had quite a big influence on me. Seeing him today in the morning, he came for the time trial after he started to feel better, it was pretty emotional at the start,' he continued.

'I was super happy to see him after a few months. I was really happy he could be here today to support me to another breakthrough.'

The questions from the media reverted back to Pogačar's performance and how his two Tour victories compared.

'Every day we went full gas this year, as we did last year. It was more or less the same,' he said diplomatically.

As Peiper alludes, that was and wasn't true.

The year before Pogačar won the Tour from Primož Roglič in the penultimate time trial.

Roglič's Jumbo–Visma squad had been so strong throughout the campaign that I had already written a column on Roglič's win. It was the first time since 2012 that I'd missed being at the Tour in person due to the pandemic and staying up until the wee hours of the morning to watch the race and report on it had taken a toll, so I filed early and went to bed.

When I awoke in Australia to see the result, it was DEFCON 1-level panic stations as I hoped against hope that my column hadn't already been published online.

Jumbo–Visma had watched as Pogačar won the time trial to rip the *maillot jaune* from Roglič's shoulders. George Bennett recalls witnessing the performance atop La Planche des Belles Filles in disbelief. There was nothing they could do.

'Primož didn't have a bad ride, he actually did a really strong ride, numerically was really powerful, one of his better TTs, all that stuff, but Pogačar just put down an absolute freakish ride that you couldn't contend with,' Bennett says.

'I mean, it was a minute faster than anybody else, even the world champ, you know. So, all we could do was watch.

'The first half of it we were sort of believing that Pogačar had just started too fast,' Bennett continues. 'And then the second time check we went, woo, all right, he's playing with the dice now, he needs to, obviously Pogačar is just going to explode when he gets to the hill or something.'

But Pogačar didn't slow down.

'We thought the time checks were wrong, but then finally when it came to the last few k [kilometres] we started to believe what we were seeing and just thought, "Okay, well, shit."'

The Jumbo–Visma riders were desolate when they arrived back at their hotel that night. Everyone had a beer, recalled funny stories from earlier in the week to improve morale and then the next day rode into Paris, fixed on trying to support Wout van Aert to a stage win.

'Then we had a big dinner and went home,' Bennett says.

It was not so much Pogačar's performances at that Tour, or the 2021 edition, that provided the biggest insight into his character, however.

In 2021, Pogačar took the yellow jersey after stage 8 and held onto it until Paris. The *maillot jaune*, regardless of how they do on a stage, is required to speak to the press every day, so we saw him a lot. In Saint-Émilion there was more time to allow for reflection and Pogačar was asked to name his favourite moment of what had been an emphatic Tour.

He had a multitude of moments to choose from.

He could have said another yellow jersey, or any of the fancies of a young, successful man. He could have referred to his stage 5 win, a 27.2-kilometre time trial from Change to Laval. He could have mentioned his first victory in the Pyrenees, racing to Col de Portet where he celebrated solo, or his three-way sprint against Jonas Vingegaard and Richard Carapaz to Luz Ardiden. His team had not planned on him going for that one.

'I called Andrej after Luz Ardiden and I said, "Was it the plan to win the stage today?" Because really, he could just sit back, follow, finish and win the Tour,' Peiper says.

'And Andrej said, "No, no, he wanted to win today at all costs."

'He said to me with a laugh, "You know our son, we can't say anything to him, he just does what he wants."

'And that's it, that's Tadej. He's so spontaneous. He just wants to race. He just wants to get out there and attack and have fun. As long as he can keep that spirit, I think he'll be up there for a very long time.'

Pogačar's spirit came through when he answered the question about his favourite moment.

'One of the favourites was the win on Col de Portet after such teamwork,' he said.

'And also today, before the start, seeing Allan Peiper.'

It was a personal and profound response from someone who has already achieved so much but also seems to be just getting started, always looking for the next win.

Much has been said about the people around Pogačar. A handful of pundits have been keen to point out that some of them have dirty pasts. I'm not familiar with any of them or well-versed in their history.

But the personal rapport Pogačar has with mentors like Peiper and Hauptman, who as a Slovenian national team coach he has known him for a long time, also says something, more wholesome, about him and his development.

'He's just very talented,' Peiper says. 'He was riding his bike already when he was a little kid and Andrej actually took him to his first race when he was eleven or twelve years old, just a little tiny guy. Andrej said, "Just go and have some fun," and he won the bike race.

'It flowered from there,' Peiper continues.

'He's got a really good family. His mother is a French teacher, they're really grounded people. He said he's got a good home life, a good family and that gives him a good basis.'

Stability and a sense of protection, or belonging, have been perhaps two of Pogačar's biggest advantages in ascending the throne.

Chris Froome partly attributed a stable home life to his transformation into a prolific Grand Tour contender. Richie Porte pulled off one of his best performances at the race when he felt like his teammates doubled as bodyguards.

'He's just a really respectful kid,' Peiper says.

'That's all it is. It comes down to respect. I think when you get that from such a top rider it can only go back again. I don't chase after him but he's always so grateful for anything that gets done for him.'

As a sports director, Peiper was always keen to and did help young athletes realise their possibilities and goals.

'And that doesn't have to be the champions,' he says.

'I get, regularly, messages from riders who were lower tiered thanking me for years ago when I looked after them, giving them the right program.

'I think that's where it comes from, that wanting to be of service to the riders. Not looking for your own personal glory, because that's not the right way of looking at anything. If it's meant to come to you, it will. But focusing on the riders and being there for them, that's the big thing in this job.'

And with Pogačar, Peiper has excelled both in fostering but also preparing him for what's to come.

'Tadej likes to laugh,' Peiper says.

'He's improved his talking on screen and on camera; cleaned it up and [is] taking time to talk and thinking through things and not getting riled by questions.

'But also, that's a part of his playful attitude. He's not going to be bullied into a corner, he's not going to be put down by insinuations.

'It would be a pity if he had to give that up to play the political game of keeping other people happy in the sport. As long as he can keep winning, why wouldn't he? Maybe it will work against him in the long run in the Tour de France, but he's such a likeable guy it shouldn't.'

CHAPTER 16
SUPER TEAMS

For the better part of a decade, the former Sky and now Ineos Grenadiers team had beaten its Tour de France rivals into near total submission.

The slick British juggernaut would arrive with one leader, who had one aim, to win the yellow jersey, with the support of a unified team strong enough to bring down any rivals with laser-like precision.

Control was central to each of its successful campaigns and influenced how the Tour was raced, so much so that when Tadej Pogačar won back-to-back titles in 2020 and 2021, the Slovenian's squad was perceived by some as weak because it did not compete in the same way.

BikeExchange head sports director Matt White had seen the heavy-handed tactic once before, at the former US Postal team, where he rode for three seasons in the early 2000s.

'The professionalism, the way people prepare, and how big

teams are, the budgets and the structure is very different from 2004 to 2005,' says White.

'But, as far as the way it's raced, I think that Armstrong era, the way US Postal rode and dominated the race, if you look at Ineos, they have copy and pasted that style of racing, really.

'They were the first team to do that and first team that had enough depth to control a race or strangle a race to that degree in the modern era,' White continues.

'I don't know about the seventies and eighties. But I know in the last twenty-five to thirty years they were the first team to really do that. And Ineos had the ability and budget to keep that same style of racing.'

Even with the arrival of Pogačar, Ineos remain a force to be reckoned with.

On a material level, in 2021 the team was still said to have the biggest budget in the WorldTour, operating off an estimated €50 million (AU $77 million) per annum well ahead of UAE Emirates, which, according to website *Statista*, had the second biggest purse at €35 million (AU $54 million), with Jumbo–Visma third at €27 million (AU $41 million).

'AFL teams' budgets, it's a drop in the ocean compared to what Ineos have,' says Richie Porte.

However, Porte counters that it's not how much the team has to withdraw but rather how principal David Brailsford invests it that makes the operation so successful.

'You never see Dave drinking the most expensive bottle of wine at dinner, whereas other team managers I've been with, that's how they operate,' Porte says.

'They complain about Ineos having more money than

anyone else, yet they spend money in silly ways.

'Dave and also [Jumbo–Visma managing director] Richard Plugge, those guys are smarter with how they spend their money than the other teams and that's why they've got the best teams.'

In 2021 Ineos won the Giro d'Italia with Egan Bernal, and Geraint Thomas and Porte took turns in supporting each other to victories in the Tour.

Porte helped Thomas earlier in the season win at the Tour de Romandie, to boost the Welshman's confidence. In return, Thomas sent Porte a text message during the Criterium du Dauphiné, saying he'd go all in for the Australian. It was smart, Porte reflected in the aftermath, because he was then happy to dedicate himself to Thomas at that year's Tour.

'I wouldn't have won the Dauphiné without that team, it's just the fact of the matter,' Porte says. 'There is something very special about that team. They don't miss anything.'

The totalitarian power of the squad though had started to wane.

Chris Froome was focused on rehabilitation from a career-threatening injury, and in 2019 and 2020, his last two seasons with the squad, did not compete at the race he had for a long time reigned over. The crown rested heavily on Bernal's head in a 2020 Tour title defence, which he ended up abandoning due to a back complaint.

Without Bernal, Michał Kwiatkowski won a stage but no one from the team figured in the top ten on general classification, which prior to that Tour had been virtually unheard of. For most outfits any victory, or GC podium result, constitutes a successful campaign, but some pundits viewed

Ineos's campaign a failure, and the team management sensed change on the horizon.

The practices that once set Ineos Grenadiers apart became somewhat universal. The industry had caught up to its 'marginal gains'.

Everyone bought into high altitude training, which aids depth.

'It doesn't give you more power but it gives you the ability to repeat the power,' says George Bennett.

'Or, if you've got three hard climbs, you'll be able to do the same power on the third climb as the first climb.'

Training techniques, which became more specific than clocking up hundreds of 'dead' kilometres on the road as well as aerodynamics, made the peloton faster. Pogačar hit the scene with UAE Team Emirates and Jumbo–Visma came of age with a strong work ethic and smart recruitment strategy, including staff with a proven record in rider development.

There'd also been big personnel changes within Ineos Grenadiers' inner sanctum, some of which cut deep, had a reverberating effect, and altered the feel of the squad from management to rider rosters. The nucleus of the team, once comprised largely of British riders, became more international. There were no native English speakers in the team that supported Bernal to triumph at the Giro.

'It's not the same team as Sky,' Porte says. 'With Sky, we had a bunch of guys who lived in Monaco, were all trained by Tim Kerrison and we were mates on and off the bike. Not to say that it's not the same now, but it is very different.'

The peloton had evolved too. The new generation were not intimidated by the hierarchy of older riders, or even really concerned with the media. They didn't subscribe to the concept of earning your stripes and then calling the shots. They just called the shots.

In his second Tour in 2018, Primož Roglič was so focused that getting insights from him about his character or his thoughts on the race, which he finished fourth overall, was about as easy as acquiring blood from a stone.

On a rest day that year I'd asked an NBC cameraman what he made of the former ski-jumper. In my job everything largely boils down to personality. Some people you will click with and others you just won't and are never going to get a good interview from them.

So, with Roglič, I figured maybe it was just me. Maybe the NBC crew was able to glean something from him that I could not. They didn't.

After the 2018 Tour, I met Roglič again, at the Tour of Britain a couple months later where the atmosphere was more relaxed. There, he seemed to recognise me, was welcoming and spoke openly and eloquently. The next season anti-doping officials told me and a *Velonews* colleague that he was a natural comedian when he visited them to do mandated tests during races. And now at the Tour he's as chatty as he was that day in Britain.

As the new faces became more comfortable, the establishment, being Ineos Grenadiers, was finally challenged, and control gave way to organised chaos. This contributed to a perceived sense of lawlessness in the peloton, which White touched on after a spate of crashes in the first week of the 2021 Tour.

'This is the biggest event of the year and people are all just looking out for themselves, that's one thing,' White says.

'And talking to our guys in the bus as well, there is a general lack of respect for each other in the peloton. There are guys who are taking a lot of risks.

'You hear stories from the guys of people pushing each other out of the way, grabbing each other. That didn't fly that long ago. So, when the trend is that's acceptable it also heightens the danger.'

Those assaults are hard to see unless you're in the peloton, but riders talking in pairs and shaking their heads in apparent disbelief as they crossed the finish lines of stages was plain to see.

According to Simon Clarke it isn't a lack of respect between riders, which he says has been on a downward trend that has changed the tempo. Rather, just how much the team leading the Tour influences the way in which the competition is run and won.

'Basically,' Clarke says, 'there is much less control [now].'

Clarke at the 2021 Tour found that when UAE Team Emirates assumed the yellow jersey after stage 8 onwards, and didn't lead from the very front, as Ineos always had, the racing became much more difficult.

'The UAE style is to sit back and let the other teams figure out who is going to go in the break and then they'd just take over after that,' Clarke says.

'As a result, everyone tries to get in the break and, also, being a little bit less dominant of a team, there's kind of that sense that every team thinks they can maybe flick UAE by getting in the breakaway and putting them on the back foot.

'But so far,' Clarke continues, 'I don't believe they're as

weak as other people think they are. So far, they've proved that they're actually quite a strong team.'

Porte also noted the change under Pogačar.

'When you had a Chris Froome, who was the strongest guy in the race at the time, it was much easier to be here and to do your job,' Porte says.

'If you're riding the tempo on the front, it's much easier doing that than being there, trying to stay in the bunch. It's easier to hurt yourself probably than have someone else hurt you, put it that way.'

Porte was not among those who suggested Pogačar didn't have a strong team behind him, either.

'They showed they are a very strong team and they've ridden really well,' he says.

'Obviously having the head-and-shoulders strongest guy in the race makes it easier but there's just no control in the starts and it's absolutely hectic. It's not their fault. The roads have also been hard to control on: uphill stages, downhill, wet descents and stuff like that, it's not an easy race to control.'

It was an observation that Froome himself echoed when he returned to the Tour in 2021 also in an unfamiliar position. The four-time champion was not the commander-in-chief of an empire, rather a marquee face at his new team Israel Start-Up Nation, which was embarking on only its second race participation.

Being at the Tour that year, even if it was to persevere at the back of the peloton, was big-picture beneficial and Froome put ego aside and channelled his ruthless conviction into that.

'The last couple of years, or last handful of years, there was always one team that was very dominant in terms of controlling the peloton,' Froome says, indirectly talking about himself and the stable he rose to prominence with.

'This year the style, not saying that UAE haven't been strong enough to do it but saying that the style in which they control the race has been very different.'

How Pogačar competed during the 2021 Tour was somewhat emblematic of that. Sporadic.

In the second week the winners of mountain stages invariably came from breakaways, racing ahead of Pogačar and his team, which stayed with the main group where another contest unfolded.

In press conferences, Pogačar routinely defended the strength of his squad as it was questioned and criticised.

It got to a point where I asked Pogačar in a post-stage press conference, before the race hit its climax in the Pyrenees, if he had any interest in going for another stage win.

'I already won a stage on time trial, so I'm really happy with that,' Pogačar answered.

'The team is working super hard to keep me in yellow. Maybe sometimes I can do a mistake to go for the stage and burn all my matches from the team, so the first goal is to defend the yellow.'

At the time I took that at face value. No, he wasn't going to. But in hindsight he foretold what would happen next.

Five days out from the finish of that Tour, presumably when Pogačar felt it was safest to do so, he flipped the switch and let rip in the Pyrenees to firmly cement who was boss.

Maybe the Tour would have run differently had his marquee rivals – the likes of Roglič and Thomas – not paid a heavy price for crashes they were involved in during the first week.

'A lot of GC riders lost out in that first week,' Froome says. 'I'd say a good fifty per cent of all GC riders were written off already, just with their injuries and crashes in the first week.'

But the fact Pogačar was one of few contenders who did not come down in the crash-marred race was a feat that spoke to the vigilance of his team. And they got the job done. Pogačar won three stages and finished the Tour with more than five minutes on runner-up Jonas Vingegaard and Richard Carapaz.

'I think our team has come of age in the last year,' Peiper says. 'We had not such a strong team and a bit of bad luck last year [2020], with riders being injured. We got through the Tour and won it in a spectacular manner but this year we had to step up and be a fully-fledged team.

'I think the doubters saying we weren't strong enough, I think those comments have been put to bed.'

Brailsford had anticipated the shift from control to organised chaos well before Pogačar's second victory and, on the eve of the 2021 season, put a positive spin on change.

'The second half of [2020] the racing was different, we found ourselves in different circumstances where we raced differently,' Brailsford had reflected.

'And people loved it, people thrived on it, the riders thrived on it, throughout the whole team the level of performances lifted and it's a really interesting thing to explore.'

There was no talk of reinstating order and control at the Tour, and he also did not dwell on the end of an era with Froome. Brailford's team would adapt to unpredictable and open racing.

'There's something about the willingness to take and create those opportunities where the racing opens up. That's the approach we're going to take,' he'd said.

'Equally, we're not reckless. The greatest, charismatic racers of all time, they won a lot, but they were clever. They're not naïve in how they would use themselves, or not reckless with it, so I think that's got to be borne in mind as well.'

That's actually exactly what Pogačar did.

Ineos Grenadiers entered the Tour with four leaders, not one, which Froome observes was something the squad hadn't done when he was previously involved.

'It's been a completely different race for them,' Froome says.

But as the Tour progressed the team at times appeared to revert to its old playbook, from trying to take control of the main group and improve Carapaz's place on GC, to wrangling with the different style of play, which appeared natural to the Ecuadorian but less so to those supporting him.

According to Thomas, how the squad was racing wasn't a reflection of being under the thumb of UAE Team Emirates, or a fresh approach but was due to Carapaz.

'Billy [Carapaz] is a completely different rider to what I was,' he said at the start of stage 15.

'If I was there [up on general classification] it would be different, I guess, because what we've done in the past is what works best for me, and Brad and Froomey.

'Whereas now Billy, Egan as well to an extent, [it's] different riders, pure climbers, *puncheurs*, who can race a bit differently.'

Ineos Grenadiers lost road captain Rowe after he missed the time cut on stage 11, which featured a double ascent of Mont Ventoux, but Thomas maintained that was a result of a freak day for his compatriot, not the team doing something Pogačar was mindful of in his own campaign: burning matches.

'Here it's a funny one though because you don't want to get drawn into doing all the work for UAE,' Thomas said, 'but at the same time you want to make sure he [Carapaz] jumps up onto the podium and he obviously needs a bit of a buffer for the TT [penultimate stage].

'So, you don't want to lose hope on winning but at the same time you need to remember you've got to move up on GC first anyway.'

Thomas had felt like absolute crap in that pursuit carrying crash-related injuries.

'It's definitely all in the head when it comes to injuries,' he'd said. 'It makes a huge difference where your mind is at.'

On the flat stages, he'd be out the back suffering in echelons not of his own making.

'And then when I had a job to be up there, trying to help [classics specialist] Dylan [van Baarle] get in the break, you feel a lot better because you feel like you're in the race, rather than swinging out the arse,' Thomas said.

'[You] know that you're definitely not going to be up there on GC, but you can still help the team and maybe get a chance yourself at some point as well.'

It was a more opportunistic outlook for an empire forced to divide its territory into kingdoms and now fight for, not defend, the throne.

CHAPTER 17
SIGHT FOR SORE EYES

I t's different, Paris, to the rest of the Tour.

Most of the Tour is comprised of country roads or old market towns. You cut through purple lavender crops that lightly perfume the air, and bright sunflower fields. You take in wild green grass that now covers the final resting places of World War I and II soldiers on flat plains. Religious crosses signal the entry and exit points of tiny stone villages, all which feature a chapel, if not a cathedral.

There are bigger cities, too. Like Brest, which is full of Irish bars. Then there are the supermarket carparks where a lot of stages start, farmland dotted with hay bales and the sides of imposing mountains so steep you must concentrate to not lose your balance, or your breath, in the thin air that can turn from hot to icy cold as clouds barrel across the sky almost in an instant.

In 2021 I arrived in Paris having watched the peloton clock 3414 kilometres of racing across twenty-one stages, the shortest of which was 108 kilometres and the longest a testing 249 kilometres. The longest Tour in the last ten years was the 2017 edition, which was 3540 kilometres long.

Those of us on the Tour never really get a chance to properly see a lot of the sights, like the chateaus some viewers tune in for.

But when you reach Paris, with its grandeur and nuance, all the torment of the Tour, all the tension, washes away. You feel like you've returned to civilisation and don't even mind the smog, the smoking, or the rude wait staff.

Richie Porte says there are a lot of egos in the peloton, but in Paris they subside, if only for a moment.

'We all have an ego and that's why we're professional sportsmen,' Porte says. 'There are quite a lot of tussles but the ongoing joke is that you get to Paris, and you ride into Paris, and you all kind of see someone and say, "Sorry I called you a whatever on stage six."'

The general classification is decided by then but for the sprinters the twenty-first and final stage is their last chance to secure a victory. The stage traditionally finishes on the Champs-Élysées, which is completely closed off to traffic for the race.

The start of the stage changes location every year and is ceremonial. Riders appear rejuvenated; they smile, creases from sleep erased from their faces. The classification leaders come to the front for a photo op, resplendent in fresh yellow, green, white, and polka-dot jerseys.

I rarely go to the start of the last stage but did at my first Tour in 2012 when I covered it on the motorbike.

On the road the teams weren't in their own enclaves or

formation as usual, they'd split up with riders from rival squads talking jubilantly in pairs. I felt like I was crashing a boys' night and asked my driver to take me to the finish.

We were flying by the time we hit the cobbles that distinguish the finishing straight the peloton completes multiple laps of. After a couple of laps, well ahead of the bunch on the bike, I bid my driver adieu and found a position by the overarching gantry that signalled the end of the Tour.

Every year three jets fly over in a spectacular formation, leaving a trail of coloured red, blue and white smoke in the sky as the riders enter the finishing circuit. Their wrists slightly jar over the beige cobbles, stained with the pollution of traffic, and haphazardly covered by bitumen in places.

Smiles and niceties give way once more to concentration and competition as the peloton strings out into single file, powering towards the Arc de Triomphe and then back towards the Place de la Concorde.

'As soon as the racing starts again, when you get into Paris, anyone that says the last stage of the Tour is a procession has never done the Tour because it's really not, then they're flicking each other again,' Porte continues.

'At the end of the day, most guys in the peloton, they'll have problems with someone and then end up being teammates with them and get on like a house on fire. It's just how it is. No different to any office.'

Riding into Paris was always a buzz for Robbie McEwen, but the first time especially.

'Seeing the Eiffel Tower, coming onto the Champs-Élysées, that was incredible,' he says.

'The first time I got goosebumps. There was a lot of

excitement, and I wasn't one of the favourites, I'd been struggling to be in the top five.'

For McEwen the final stage was never a ceremonial procession because, no matter how successful the previous weeks had been, as a sprinter he still had a lot to lose in Paris.

'I was always trying to win and that was the last opportunity and there was always a lot riding on that last day: stage win, possible green jersey,' McEwen says.

'So, I never went into Paris relaxed. I never got to enjoy the day because the enjoyment of the day hinged on the result.

'If I won, it was like, "What a great day that was," and if I lost it was like, "Meh."'

The finish line is about halfway between the Place de la Concorde, near where the teams' paddock is assembled, and the Arc de Triomphe, which forms the background to the podium that is quickly assembled after the stage is run and done.

The riders will come to a halt just past the finish line and take a moment. They gather with their teammates, shaking hands, high-fiving and hugging each other in a mark of congratulatory respect. They pose for photos and see their close friends and family. For me, the Tour is the one race on the calendar where, come the end of it, you really do just want to see those who matter to you.

In the immediate aftermath of the final stage the teams' paddock is buzzing, with riders, staff, their friends and family, media and some fans all mingling. In 2019 Michał Kwiatkowski just sat on the ground outside the Ineos Grenadiers bus, still in his kit, eating a slice of pizza from the box in front of him and washing it down with a beer.

At sunset the teams move on, and organisers start to pack

away the gantry and reopen the Champs-Élysées to traffic once more. Nearby bars are closed for private parties though many of them were open to the public in 2021. That year, France had emerged from tough lockdown restrictions only weeks earlier, and a lot of riders competing at the Tokyo Olympics left for Japan that night or the next morning.

People say they swear off ever doing the Tour again the day it finishes but I don't think anyone takes for granted standing on the Champs-Élysées.

Mathew Hayman recalls travelling to Paris with his father as a teenager to watch the Tour finish. He was a successful amateur racing rider in Europe then and believed he would be on the other side of the fence in no time.

'I was racing over here [Europe] with the amateur team and broke my collarbone so was off for a while. My dad had come over to visit and we took a bus from Holland down to see the stage on the Champs-Élysées,' Hayman recalls.

Father and son woke up at 4.30 am to get the bus and found a spot near the Arc de Triomphe, where they stood for hours.

'We watched the cars going around and watched the riders and it was pretty amazing, the crowd was ten deep,' he says.

'I was pretty cocky, and I said, "Oh look, Dad, next time I'll be on that side of the fence; there's way too many people on this side of the fence."'

Hayman and his father got back home around 1 am; it was a long day but the journey to the other side of the fence would be even longer. More than a decade later he recounted that visit as a spectator to team owner Gerry Ryan as they both stood on the other side of the fence after Hayman had just finished his first Tour.

'I told him however many years ago it was that I'd stood up there and said as a cocky eighteen-year-old, "Next time I come back I'll be on that side of the fence." And it took me that long to actually get there,' Hayman says.

'It was a massive thing the first time just to finish, to say, "Look, I've done the Tour de France" and you can finally call yourself a rider. Even though I'd won Roubaix before that, it still meant a great deal to me to get to the finish in Paris.'

It was an especially great deal to Cadel Evans the year he won the yellow jersey in 2011 but the warhorse was so scared of jinxing the result that he asked his BMC team not to plan a party.

'You'd think we'd have a big party but, funnily enough, the year before, when I lost, they'd organised a big party, hoping that I would win. And for me, it was a complete letdown because you're jinxing me,' Evans recalls.

'They had to organise the party before I'd taken the jersey because I'm always trying to take the jersey on the last stage because I didn't have the team to defend the jersey if I did take it earlier.'

So when Evans won yellow, he attended a team function for employees and sponsors, but no other celebration had been planned. There was no lavish party at a fancy establishment. Instead, the team that supported him to victory returned to their hotel.

Despite being one of the biggest metropolises in the world, Paris is a city that likes to sleep. Hospitality services close early on Sunday nights, when the Tour finishes, and most places are shut Mondays.

'The French hotel didn't have any cold beer. Here we are,

sitting down there, just won the Tour de France and the French hotel didn't have any more cold beer,' says Evans.

He realised that everyone was at the hotel except for George Hincapie, so he called the American.

'George, where are you?'

'I'm buying pizza on the Champs-Élysées.'

'Can you get ten?'

Hincapie returned with a dozen pizzas, and everyone tucked in.

'We just sat there together in complete happiness and satisfaction. Yeah, the beer was warm, but what do you expect?' says Evans.

Every year I can see in photos taken on the Champs-Élysées that I look five to ten years older compared to when I started the Tour. I've lost weight and one eye appears lazy. I sleep virtually uninterrupted for three days to one week afterwards. When my friends and family see me arriving home to the UK or Australia, lugging a massive red suitcase around, they look upon my face with sympathy.

'How was the Tour?' they ask.

The day after, my reply is always the same as the riders.

'I fucking hate the Tour de France,' I say.

But I don't.

It's almost a cliché now how many people swear off the Tour the day, or the day after, it finishes and then so soon after have an eye to the next one.

Not even Chris Froome took his return to the race in 2021 for granted.

'I'm going to keep working as hard as I can and I'm extremely grateful to be here this time around,' he said.

The Tour brings out the best and petulant worst in you, sometimes in the same day, and while there are some who have chosen not to return, some who don't rate it, there are more who build their lives around the race. There are journalists who have reported from the Tour since before I was born in 1986 and they are present every year, still hooked.

George Bennett remembers the build-up to the delayed 2020 Tour as being intense beyond imagination. He went from being at home for a bit to not at all. Bennett had left home for a training camp, from which he went straight to the Vuelta a Burgos in July and from there to the Tour de l'Ain in August.

'Then I drove across straight to Italy for a week, then we drove back to altitude, then we went to the Tour,' Bennett says.

'It had been like two-and-a-half months with these guys, or three months, in a bubble, together, on the road all for this one thing.

'In the end, like win or lose, I was happy to be out of there,' Bennett continues.

'I loved it, it was an amazing experience, but I just also wanted to sit on my couch, not look at the food coach app. You know, I was just done with it.

'I think the fact that we didn't win probably also compounded that: "Right, time to get out of here and [back to] my own space for a few weeks before I get back with the boys."'

The Tour de France is not glamorous. It's warm beer, not cold champagne; it's months of isolation and starvation, not A-list parties and fine dining; it's working around the clock for prize money that hasn't increased in more than a decade; it's sacrificing your own dreams sometimes for those of another, or shouldering the pressure of an entire squad under a spotlight that can build you up as quickly as it can tear you down. It's highway motels mixed with twelfth-century chateaus; it's being exposed to the elements and operating at extremes often out of your control.

Prior to the COVID-19 pandemic, access at the Tour was very open. At one of the biggest sporting events on the planet, everyone in the industry still knows each other by name.

There are an infinite number of stories that come out of the Tour every day but only a handful are ever told.

Central to them all though is not money or glory, or even records. It's passion, heart and quaint, old-school nuances.

The day after the Tour de France finishes nearly everyone who has competed in it will tell you they hate it. But they don't. They love it. No, actually, they fucking love it.

AFTERWORD

The Tour de France is the world's biggest annual sporting contest, steeped in rich history and legend. It's enticing to look back at the memories I've made reporting on this prestigious race. I've watched some of the best athletes to have lived compete while staying in towns built by Romans; I've sipped champagne in Champagne. On the other hand, I've posed by war statues metres inland from Utah Beach where, thinking of D-day, smiling did not feel appropriate.

But now I want to look to the future, specifically at the Tour de France Femmes avec Zwift.

One hundred and nineteen years after cyclist and journalist Henri Desgrange founded the first Tour de France, a women's Tour will return for the first time in over three decades.

Race organiser, ASO and race director, Marion Rousse hopes the Tour de France Femmes will do what the three past iterations have not: endure.

The eight-stage race begins in Paris on July 24, 2022, when

the men's Tour finishes, and concludes in the Vosges Mountains on July 31, paying homage to antiquity and lore en route.

'From the foundation of the past and present of the Tour de France, the riders at the Tour de France Femmes avec Zwift, will write their own history,' says Rousse.

Women's cycling has faced an uphill battle, with conflicting changes in governance, poor pay and planning, shoestring budgets, abuse and exposure among the chief problems.

Now, a keen public interest, and progress, from professionalism to increased (but still not perfect) parity, has become hard to ignore.

There's arguably never been a better time for the Tour de France Femmes. Here's to people talking about the pain and privilege of that race's competitors for the next century too.

ACKNOWLEDGEMENTS

Thank you to my dad, Alan, and my mum, Sharon, for everything. To my partner, Noel, sister, Madeline, and brothers Benjamin and Gregory for keeping me on track.

Thank you so much to Richie Porte, Michael Matthews, Cadel Evans, Chris Froome, Marcel Kittel, Sam Bennett, Robbie McEwen, Caleb Ewan, Matt White, Mathew Hayman, George Bennett, Simon Clarke, Luke Durbridge, Enrico Poitschke, Michael Mørkøv, Cameron Meyer and Jens Debusschere for letting me 'get under your skin' at a time when the world was scared and disjointed, and communicating was difficult. And to all the other athletes, teams, media colleagues and industry parties who have enriched my knowledge of and experiences at the Tour – you know you are. To Seb Piquet, Martijn Redegeld, James Forsyth, Paul Nevin, Kurt Van Roosbroeck and Matt Rabin for your insights.

Thank you to George Solomon, Ralph Scherzer, Lucy Martin, Geoffrey Pizzorni, Mikkel Conde, Michelle Froome,

Phil Lowe, Frédéric Adam, Fabrice Tiano and Ard Bierens for making the interview process easier.

Thank you to Daniel Benson, Chloe Saltau, Wade Pearce, Jim Bruce-Ball, Jeremy Whittle and William Fotheringham for keeping me employed around and being flexible with the demands of this project, and for the ongoing interest of other commissioners.

And finally, thank you to Ultimo Press, James Kellow, Brigid Mullane, Deonie Fiford, Alisa Ahmed, Alissa Dinallo and Ronnie Scott for coming to me with the opportunity to write my first book, for sharing my enthusiasm, passion and interest in cycling, and for all your fantastic work and patience. This has been the most challenging project of my career to date but a great privilege I learned a lot from and can only hope to improve on.

Sophie Smith is a freelance journalist and broadcaster with 14 years of experience reporting for commercial newspapers, magazines, websites and television. Sophie has a background in international and Olympic sports, and got hooked on professional cycling when she was assigned the round as a cadet. She spent two years living and working for cycling titles in London, exclusively following the WorldTour circuit. Now based in inner-city Melbourne, every year Sophie travels across the world to cover professional races for major Australian, UK and US press outlets. The 35-year-old has reported from nine Tours de France and counting, four UCI Road World Championships, the Giro d'Italia, spring classics, London 2012, the UCI Track World Championships, Tour Down Under, Tour of California, Tour of Britain, UAE Tour, Tour of Oman and more. She has a Bachelor of Arts degree from Monash University where she majored in journalism.